Journal of the Fantastic in the Arts
—The Fantastic is the Allegory of the Actual—

Volume 36/ Number 3
Whole Number 121
Supported by the
International Association for the Fantastic in the Arts.

JFA

Journal of the Fantastic in the Arts
—The Fantastic is the Allegory of the Actual—

Volume 36/ Number 3
Whole Number 121
Supported by the
International Association for the Fantastic in the Arts.

FAVIAN PRESS

A FAVIAN PRESS PAPERBACK

© Copyright 2025
JFA

The right of JFA to be identified as author of this work has been asserted in accordance with the Copyright, Designs and Patents Act 1988

All Rights Reserved

No reproduction, copy or transmission of the publication may be made without written permission. No paragraph of this publication may be reproduced, copied or transmitted save with the written permission of the publisher, or in accordance with the provisions of the Copyright Act 1956 (as amended).

Any person who does any unauthorised act in relation to this publication may be liable to criminal prosecution and civil claims for damages.

ISBN 978 1 78695 916 4

Published by Favian Press
an imprint of Fiction4All
www.fiction4all.com

This edition published 2025

Editors-in-Chief *Submissions*	Tedd Hawks
Managing	Jude Wright
Production	Cat Ashton
Production Assistant	Miranda Miller
Acquisitions and Reviews	Novella Brooks de Vita
Senior Submissions and Reviews Editor	Farah Mendlesohn
Peer Review Editor	Ida Yoshinaga
Accessibility & Sensitivity Coordinator	Alexis Brooks de Vita
Regional Submissions, Accessibility, Sensitivity & Reviews Editors	Taryne Taylor Sang-Keun Yoo
Editor-at-Large	Dale Knickerbocker

COVER ART
Tchoodi le murmure
Malian French painter and illustrator Jenekacy is inspired by African, Afro-descendant spiritualities and the quest for oneself, seeking through her works to reveal what is hidden, to make accessible to all those who contemplate invisible worlds, present as much inside only outside of us and to tell legends which are perhaps not in the end.

Also passionate about fantasy and lore, Jenekacy creates new worlds largely inspired by her own understanding of the current world. Her colorful universe depicts this search for identity through varied archetypes imbued with mysticism, where ancestors, deities and spirits are never far away. It is an ode to her multicultural roots and to life in general.

Jenekacy's work can be found online at
https://jenekacy.jimdosite.com/

and Instagram
https://www.instagram.com/jenekacy_art/

GENERAL INQUIRIES
Inquiries and other editorial correspondence should be directed to journal@fantastic-arts.org.

SUBMISSIONS
Like the International Conference on the Fantastic in the Arts, *JFA* welcomes papers on all aspects of the fantastic in world literatures and media, as well as interdisciplinary approaches including African/Diaspora Studies, anthropology, area studies, critical game studies, disability studies, future studies, gender studies, history, Indigenous studies, music, philosophy, political science, postcolonial studies, psychology, queer studies, religious studies, science and technology studies, and sociology. All papers are made available in English and fully refereed. The journal is indexed in the MLA Bibliography.

Submissions should contain a more in-depth discussion than a conference-length paper and demonstrate a grasp of current scholarship on the subject. The length of articles generally varies from 3,500-9,000 words and ranges from 15-35 pages.

All submissions are peer-reviewed in accordance with our peer review statement, the *Submission, Accessibility and Sensitivity Review Handbook*, and the BIPOC Anti-Racist Statement on Scholarly Reviewing Practices. If submissions are flagged at any point of the review process for the risk of promulgating potentially misrepresentative, stereotypical, ableist, or racist views, contributors will be asked to address these problems before the review process can continue.

Since the refereeing process is anonymous, the author's name should not appear anywhere on the text file itself, including the notes. No title page is needed. However, an abstract of 100-150 words must be inserted at the beginning of each submission, clearly stating what contribution the essay makes to the study of the fantastic.

Please ensure that all citations and the Works Cited entries are in current MLA style. Please do not use automatically generated notes; end notes (only) must be entered manually. A paper that doesn't meet our printing parameters can take many hours to adjust. To avoid needless changes and delays, it is best to use our guidelines from the start. For complete guidelines, please refer to the *Submission, Accessibility and Sensitivity Review Handbook* and the *JFA In-House Style Guide*. In case of conflicting instructions, defer to the *Submission, Accessibility and Sensitivity Review Handbook* and the *JFA In-House Style Guide*. Contributors are responsible for acquiring all permissions to quote and/or use illustrations that accompany their article, and for paying (or arranging to have their institutions pay) all usage fees, including copyright.

Due to the need to provide the journal in multiple formats, the journal does not currently publish images/illustrations in articles.

Scholarly articles should be directed to the *JFA*'s Acquisitions and Reviews team (under Editor-in-Chief Novella Brooks de Vita at jfa.acquisitions@fantastic-arts.org). Please send your anonymized submission to the Submissions Editor, Tedd Hawks, at journal@fantastic-arts.org and include "ATTN: JFA Article Submission" at the start of your subject line. Allow thirty days for confirmation of receipt before querying.

BOOK REVIEWS

JFA also publishes reviews of scholarly works addressing the fantastic, broadly construed. Reviews of fiction are limited to reissues of speculative works with new introductions and scholarly apparatuses, and speculative works with the potential to impact scholarship in the genre. Books and other media received are advertised on the IAFA discussion list (which can be subscribed to through the IAFA homepage at www.iafa.org), and IAFA members are encouraged to suggest titles for review.

To mail book copies for review and for queries or reviews of English-language publications, please contact the *JFA* at journal@fantastic-arts.org.

Contents

"Funhouse or Madhouse: Whimsy in Creativity":
ICFA 45 Guests of Honor C.E. Murphy and Mary A. Turzillo,
Distinguished Scholar Mame Bougouma Diene,
Moderator Novella Brooks de Vita   1
   Geoffrey A. Landis, Transcriber

Whimsy and Social Control in Northern Senegal   7
   Woppa Diallo, Co-Distinguished Scholar, ICFA 2024
   Translated by Alexis Brooks de Vita

Imaginary Amendments and Executive Orders:
The *Noirum* and Race in United States Science Fiction   14
   Isiah Lavender III, Distinguished Scholar, ICFA 2023

Whimsy & Revolution:
A Comparative Analysis of the Works of
Marcos, Herzl and Young   35
   Mame Bougouma Diene, Co-Distinguished Scholar, ICFA 2024

Biological Haunting:
An Interview with Silvia Moreno-Garcia on
Adaptation, Genre, Eugenics, and Fungi   45
   Interviewed by Taryne Jade Taylor and Karina A. Vado

Wole Talabi's Plenary Address and Interview:
Afro-Communitarianism as a Positive Framework for Artificial
Intelligence in "A Dream of Electric Mothers"   76

Creative Think Piece—A Breath of Life:
The Necessary Human Touch in Music
An Interview of Nancy Menk, DMA, and Jason Oby, DM   92
   Interviewed by Novella Brooks de Vita

Contents

REVIEWS

Alec Nevala-Lee's *Collisions:
A Physicist's Journey from Hiroshima
to the Death of the Dinosaurs*   112
    Rev. by Geoffrey Alan Landis

Stacy Alaimo's *The Abyss Stares Back:
Encounters with Deep-Sea Life*   115
    Rev. by Supriya Baijal

"Funhouse or Madhouse: Whimsy in Creativity": ICFA 45 Guests of Honor C.E. Murphy and Mary A. Turzillo, Distinguished Scholar Mame Bougouma Diene, Moderator Novella Brooks de Vita

Geoffrey A. Landis, Transcriber

OPENING PANEL, March 13, 2024:

Novella Brooks de Vita: Whimsy: funhouse or madhouse? And why?

C.E. Murphy: The obvious answer is both. For me, it's the funhouse; that's where I love what whimsy does. It's the absurdity, the silliness, the joy of embracing whatever nonsense; but underneath, the madness makes me enthusiastic about the whimsy and our whole genre, in general. We try to say something political, something important, but we use elves, we use aliens and monsters. It's the fun of it that's so irresistible, and always has been.

Mary A. Turzillo: This has been the consummation of a dream for me. When I was a little girl, I overheard my grandmother say, "She's funny, isn't she?" and I think she meant it in a good way. I've always been whimsical. Whimsy is everything. I keep thinking yes, there's this, and there's this, and everything in-between.

Mame Bougouma Diene: This is my first convention, and my imposter syndrome is through the roof. Growing up, my introduction to the fantastic and the whimsical came through my parents. My father's bedtime stories, Hindu mythology, and Arthurian myths; stories about Hanuman, who confused the sun with a giant orange and tried to fly up to it and eat it. I've tried to write things more realistic, but they always turn completely crazy by page five. Blame my dad. Whimsy allows people to think about things without pointing fingers. If you manage to create that space for people, to allow people to reimagine even their own preconceptions, to examine their own preconceptions, it's not serious, but it really is. Through comedy, we can examine things that are really important. In a conference like this, we can examine things that are really important.

Novella Brooks de Vita: It allows us to examine very important stuff, to allow us to explore things that are tough, that are hard. The more ridiculous, the more lighthearted, the more intense, the more crucial the discussion is.

Mame Bougouma Diene: Most of us have seen the second part of *Dune*. It's interesting that the movie is finding such a huge audience, especially after the war on terror, the islamophobia, and here, some aspects of Islam are being presented to a greater audience: exchanging the word "Jihad" for "holy war". This is where the creative space allows for this kind of thing: we've reappropriated things in a very interesting way.

Mary A. Turzillo: I see whimsy as a kind of shock therapy, people approaching something very hurtful. It becomes so commonplace, people don't even hear it. Police shootings, for example. Sometimes if you can approach it, people see it and say we need to do something about it. It's not always that dire. My son died by suicide in 2020. He was a very funny guy, a whimsical guy. Sometimes, I find something of his, maybe an R2D2 toy, and it just seems so whimsical.

C.E. Murphy: I've been writing paranormal romance. That's not my strong suit. I write very, very silly paranormal romance; it's fun. Underneath the humor, I'm addressing something very important. Last year I wrote a story, "Some Bunny to Love," because I just loved the title. It's about a shapeshifter: she turns into a rabbit, and the rabbit is afraid of everything. The story that I wrote because I was amused by the title turned into a story about consent, about serious themes; and the story, which is quite funny, gives us that space to talk about something maybe we're not comfortable about, otherwise. I had a good time writing it and discovering that there's something underneath. There's a good amount of power in approaching things from this angle; people aren't looking for something profound but possibly find something profound underneath.

Novella Brooks de Vita: Any questions you have to ask each other?

Mary A. Turzillo: I have one for Catie. The country in which *The Queen's Bastard* exists; I identified most of the countries in it but would like to ask about some of the characters.

C. E. Murphy: It's an Elizabethan alternate world, where the main character is an imagined bastard of Queen Elisabeth. The tag line for it is "murder, betrayal, sex, and politics," not necessarily in that order.

Mame Bougouma Diene: Stacks of books: one side says romance, one paranormal romance. Paranormal romance: you want to sleep with the ghost, or not? I was talking about a dragon story I wrote recently about loneliness, and why people fall through the cracks. You don't want to sleep with the ghosts: you want to address your demons.

Novella Brooks de Vita: Mary, talk about the reading you did about cats last spring. How silly and engaging the opening was: you're swept along with the story, and then you discover it's deep. You surprised me. How do you do this? Is it just the madness of the play on words, is it revolutionarily thought-provoking, or did you say, "I have a goal?"

Mary A. Turzillo: Toxoplasmosis gondii. I'm certain I'm infected. I'm very messy; I'm very interested in clothes. Maybe I should be tested.

C.E. Murphy: I rarely have a goal. I have an idea and want to see where I go, where the story brings me. It's always somebody else who shows me themes, and I say: "Did I do that?" And then I say, "Oh, yes; I intended that all along!" I completely admire people who know what they're looking to say, and how they develop a theme around what they mean to say, and I have no idea how they do it.

Mame Bougouma Diene: I start with an idea or maybe an emotion. I feel very confident when I start to type, but thematically I'm never really sure what I'm trying to say. I have the feeling. For example, my wife is an advocate against gender-based violence. The real reason I write the story isn't to write a story about gender-based violence; I'm just trying to impress a girl. Sometimes it works.

Novella Brooks de Vita: What do you think needs more attention when it comes to whimsy? What should scholars and writers look for and give more attention to?

Mame Bougouma Diene: I've been depressive for years; meeting my wife and having daughters has made me whole. Your friends get bored, hearing you whine about depression. It would be great to find yourself in a space where you can remove yourself, and allow yourself to process your problems. That could help a lot of people.

Mary A. Turzillo: People ought to be more tolerant; I don't mean just big things, but little things, like people break up with their families over stupid little things, like whether you put the dressing on the turkey before or after you put it in the oven. Everything doesn't have to be a divide. Maybe sometimes you should just forget; you need to be able to say things that are stupid, realize people are just people. You need to talk in a way that doesn't alienate people. You don't have to mess around with the truth; you do have to say the truth, but allow people to be different. The people who voted that way aren't necessarily evil. It seems a new issue comes up every time. I have friends who don't wear masks during the pandemic. How did that happen? Half of the people think masks are okay, half think they're evil, think vaccines turn you into a Martian. They're still just people.

C.E. Murphy: I recently read an interesting novel, *At First Sight*, about a person who ends up living in a spite house. A spite house is a house built for purposes of spiting somebody else. The main character has clinical depression. It's a very kind and sympathetic depiction of somebody who is badly suffering, a rare case of when I saw that kind of depiction on the page, where people haven't experienced it or had friends or relatives who have experienced it. When it's done well, it can be really liberating, hopefully for readers, but definitely for the author, to show people they aren't alone.

In Mary's talk about acceptance of differences in small things, I'm reminded about the lucky 1000. The point is, when you find someone who doesn't know something that you think is common knowledge, you tend to smirk, but instead you should say, "You're so lucky; you're going to learn something cool today."

Novella Brooks de Vita: Last words? What should we take

into the conference or take away?

Mary A. Turzillo: Love is love; hate is bad.

Mame Bougouma Diene: This is my first time at this convention, so I say, have as great a time as you possibly can.

C.E. Murphy: I hope we all have a great time.

END

Whimsy and Social Control in Northern Senegal

Woppa Diallo, Co-Distinguished Scholar, ICFA 2024
Translation by Alexis Brooks de Vita

BONJOUR À TOUTES ET À TOUS. Et merci pour votre présence et attention. Je m'appelle Woppa Diallo, fondatrice et directrice de l'Association pour le Maintien des Filles à l'Ecole au Sénégal, une organisation qui travaille sur les violences basées sur le genre dans le but d'aider à améliorer la scolarisation des filles et leur place dans nos sociétés. Je suis ici en qualité de Co-Autrice de « A Soul of Small Places » avec mon époux Mame Bougouma Diene.

Je vais vous parler aujourd'hui du rôle du fantastique et de la magie dans nos sociétés Africaines, et plus particulièrement dans les communautés Peules du Nord Est du Sénégal d'où je viens et ou mon association opère.

On dit souvent que la science-fiction et la fantaisie, le fantastique et l'horreur ne sont pas des thématiques littéraires Africaines. Ça n'est pas forcément vrai. « A Soul of Small Places » en est une preuve. Et beaucoup d'ouvrages et de films récents marquent une vrai vitalité et intérêt pour ces genres en Afrique.

Je pensais à *La Plus Secrète Mémoire des Hommes* de Mbougar Sarr, le film Senegalo-Congalais *Saloum* et le film Sénégalais *Atlantiques*.

Si vous n'avez pas lu ou vu ces films je vous les recommande vivement.

D'autant plus qu'ils exemplifient la compréhension du fantastique dans la vie et la compréhension de la vie en Afrique. Le livre de Mbougarr Sarr, n'est pas un livre de fiction spéculative, pourtant cette vision du monde marque toutes les expériences et la famille du personnage principal.

Il en est de même dans les films susmentionnés. Même si plus typiquement « fantastiques » que *La Plus secrète Mémoire des Hommes*, ce qui les démarque est que cette fantaisie n'est pas fantastique mais réelle.

En Afrique le fantastique et le réel sont exactement la même chose. Conversement certains disent que de ce fait, l'écriture fantastique devrait être plus acceptée en Afrique. C'est une confusion de forme. Un conte fantastique irréel n'a aucun sens en Afrique, ce fantastique, cette magie ne doit pas être perçue comme autre mais comme faisant partie du quotidien des gens.

Et c'est en cela que l'Afrique se démarque de l'occident. L'occident écrit de l'horreur et de la fantaisie auxquels ils ne croient pas. Les Africains ne le distinguent pas comme genre par ce que les gens y croient. Nous croyons en nos sortilèges, nous croyons en nos esprits et nous croyons qu'ils interagissent tous les jours et tout le temps avec nous, en bien comme en mal.

Je ne vais pas vous parler plus de littérature mais de ma culture, Sénégalaise nationalement mais Peule localement.

Un exemple qui est commun à la culture de mon mari est la prohibition pour les enfants d'être dehors au crépuscule au moment de la prière du soir maghrib. Le crépuscule est une heure ou les esprits et les vivants se rencontrent et il est essentiel de protéger les enfants. Les esprits ne sont pas forcément maléfiques mais on ne sait jamais.

Si ma fille est éveillée, je peux la laisser sans surveillance tant qu'elle est à l'intérieur. Mais si elle dort, Mame Bougouma ou moi-même devons rester avec elle jusqu'à ce que le crépuscule passe.

9 • Woppa Diallo (Transl. Alexis Brooks de Vita)

La protection des enfants est primordiale, et cela se reflète également dans nos noms.

Woppa comme celui de mon mari Bougouma, sont des noms protecteurs. Woppa veut dire « Allez-vous en » en Peule, Bougouma veut dire « Je ne veux pas » en Wolof. Ce sont des noms qui sont donnés aux enfants pour les protéger du mauvais sort et des démons.

Je porte, tout comme ma fille, et mon mari aussi, des charmes protecteurs qui peuvent avoir plusieurs fonctions de protection.

Quelque chose que ma mère me dit tous les jours, parce que ma fille crie beaucoup, est que si mon enfant crie pendant la nuit, je dois crier plus fort qu'elle pour que les esprits ne lui volent pas sa voix. Jusqu'ici tout va bien.

Comme vous voyez, dans nos cultures depuis notre enfance jusqu'à notre mort nous baignons dans la magie et la fantaisie.

Certaines de ses croyances concernent directement les femmes et servent comme mécanismes de contrôle social : dans « A Soul of Small Places » le "monstre" en question, le « soukounio » est une réalité de notre culture.

Par exemple une anecdote dans mon village, est l'exemple d'une femme qui ne voulait pas croire en l'existence du Soukounio. Une dame qui se disait Soukounio lui a demandé de ramener une pastèque. Quand elle a ramené la pastèque elle lui a demandé d'ouvrir la pastèque. Quand elle l'a ouvert elle a vu qu'elle avait été mangé de l'intérieur et avec des marques de griffe.

La Soukounio lui a montré ses mains; elles étaient pleines de jus de pastèque.

Vous connaissez sûrement le soukounio a travers sa version caribéenne, le Soucouyant. Le soucouyant est associé au vampire européen et prend la forme d'une vieille femme. Chez nous le soukounio est généralement une femme, pas forcément vieille, mais c'est souvent les vieilles femmes sont accusées d'être des soukounio.

10• Woppa Diallo (Transl. Alexis Brooks de Vita)

Une prohibition qui affecte particulièrement les jeunes filles est lié aux menstruations. Si quelqu'un voit le sang de tes menstruations, cela voudra dire que tes enfants naîtront avec des déficiences mentales. Si les filles sortent quand le soleil est à son zénith, ou pendant le coucher du soleil, son utérus sera possédé et les enfants qu'elle mettra au monde seront également possédés par le démon.

Voilà, j'espère que ça aura été intéressant; est ce qu'il y a des exemples similaires dans votre culture?

Merci!

***

Hello to everyone.

And thank you for your attendance and attention. My name is Woppa Diallo, Founder and Director of the Association for Keeping Girls in School in Senegal, an organisation that works to eradicate gender-based violence with the goal of helping to improve the educational achievement of girls and their place in our societies.

I am here as the co-author of « A Soul of Small Places » with my spouse Mame Bougouma Diene. I am going to speak today about the role of the fantastic and magic in our African societies, and more particularly in the Peuls communities, also known as the Fulani, or Fula, or Fulbe, of Northeastern Senegal where I am from, and where my Association operates.

One often says that science fiction and fantasy, the fantastic and horror, are not African literary themes. This is just not true. « A Soul of Small Places » is one proof of that. And many literary works and recent films mark a real vitality and interest in these genres in Africa.

I have been thinking of *The Most Secret Memory of Men* by Mbougar Sarr, the Senegalise-Congolese film *Saloum*, and the Senegalese film *Atlantic*.

11 • Woppa Diallo (Transl. Alexis Brooks de Vita)

If you have not read this book or seen these films I heartily recommend them to you inasmuch as they exemplify the understanding of the fantastic in life and the understanding of life in Africa.

Mbougar Sarr's book is not a book of speculative fiction as much as a vision of the world that includes the experiences and the family of the principal character.

It is among the aforementioned films; even if it is more typically fantastic than *The Most Secret Memory of Men*, what differentiates them is that this fantasy is not fantastic but real.

In Africa, the fantastic and the real are exactly the same things. Conversely, some would say that because of this fact, fantastic writing should be more accepted in Africa. This is a confusion of form. An unrealistic fantastic story has no meaning in Africa, in that the fantastic, this magic, does not have to be perceived as something else but as part of the everyday life of people.

It is in this that Africa is different from the Occident. The Occident writes about horror and fantasy as if the people do not believe in them. Africans do not distinguish genre based on whether or not people believe in it. We believe in our spells, we believe in our spirits, and we believe that they interact every day and all the time with us, for good as well as for evil.

I am not going to speak with you any more about literature but of my culture, Senegalese nationally but Peul regionally.

An example that is common in my husband's culture is the prohibition against children being outside at twilight, at the moment of the evening call to prayer. Dusk is an hour when spirits and the living meet, and it is essential to protect children. Spirits are not necessarily evil, but one never knows.

If my daughter is awake, I can leave her unattended as long as she is inside. But if she is asleep, Mame Bougouma or I myself must stay with her until dusk passes.

The protection of children is paramount, and that is reflected as well in our names.

12 • Woppa Diallo (Transl. Alexis Brooks de Vita)

Woppa, like my husband's name Bougouma, is a protective name. Woppa means « Get away from here » in Fula, and Bougouma means « I do not want » in Wolof. These are names given to children to protect them from bad luck and demons.

I wear, as do my daughter and my husband, protective charms that serve in several protective ways. Something that my mother tells me these days because my daughter cries a lot is that if my child cries during the night, I must cry more loudly than she so that the spirits will not steal her voice. Up until now, this has gone well.

As you see, in our cultures from our earliest childhood until our death, we are bathed in magic and fantasy.

Certain people have beliefs that directly concern women and serve as mechanisms of social control. In « A Soul of Small Places, » the monster in question, the « soukounio, » is a reality of our culture.

For example, an anecdote in my village is the example of a woman who did not want to believe in the existence of the Soukounio. A woman believed to be a Soukounio asked her to bring a watermelon. When she had brought the watermelon, she was asked to open it. When she opened it, one could see that she [the soukounio] had already eaten the inside and left claw marks. The Soukounio showed the woman her hands, which were full of juice from the melon.

You surely know the soukounio because of its Caribbean version, the Soucouyant. The Soucouyant is associated with the European vampire and takes the form of an old woman. We normally believe the Soukounio is generally a woman, not necessarily old, but it is often the old women who are accused of being soukounios.

One prohibition that particularly affects young girls is tied to menstruation. If someone sees your menstrual blood, that means that your children will be born with mental deficiencies.

13• Woppa Diallo (Transl. Alexis Brooks de Vita)

If a girl goes out when the sun is at its zenith, or during sunset, her uterus will become possessed and the children she will give birth to will be possessed, as well, by the demon.

There, I hope that was interesting. Are there similar examples in your culture?

Thank you!

Imaginary Amendments and Executive Orders: The *Noirum* and Race in United States Science Fiction

Isiah Lavender III, Distinguished Scholar, ICFA 2023

AS MY TITLE SUGGESTS, I investigate imaginary laws in science fiction literature. I do so to provide a counternarrative offering a reassessment of American SF's involvement in the dialogue on race and racism at the crossroads of the late twentieth century and the new millennium. I look at a variety of novums and *noirums* created by African American SF writers in a rough chronological order in this presentation. To that end, I gauge the robust creative response to the idea of colorblindness across time and the possible consequences of ignoring its embedding in our social structures. Authors whose works I touch upon include Steven Barnes, Evie Shockley, Sherri L. Smith, Justina Ireland, Maurice Carlos Ruffin, and Cadwell Turnbull.

Here's the thing: while the *noirum* does not yet exist in science fiction or Afrofuturist scholarship, it is a critical race theory that enhances the more conventional tools of the social justice discipline. "In order to bring critical race theory into conversations about […] literature, media, fandom, and popular culture," as Ebony Elizabeth Thomas suggests, "counterstories, or alternative narratives, must be foregrounded" (*Dark* 10). An elegant thought, not easily executed because science fiction, largely written by White people, and more frequently White men, often presents a colorblind, even monochrome, future. From this viewpoint, knowing SF's cultural history becomes important in understanding how the genre has changed and why it is still changing as BIPOCs imagine their own futures. We must first recognize a longstanding master narrative in SF—Black and Brown people have no future. This story has been written so often, has been viewed on the silver screen so often, has been multiply repeated so often that some people have come to believe it—namely White people. Consequently, we must learn to excavate race from the genre's "Blackground" (Lavender 6).[1] This term spotlights the deep-rooted perceptions of race and racism; it brings both the unintentional and deliberate prejudices, stereotypes, and antagonisms to our conscious attention so that we may begin telling counter-stories. As Richard Delgado proclaims, "stories can shatter complacency and challenge the status quo" ("Storytelling" 72). Then and only then can we challenge a monochrome world view by "listening to the voices of people of color as the basis for understanding how race and racism function" (Cook and Dixson 1243). Essentially, the *noirum* provides a way of seeing a particular type of counter-story, unlocking it for CRT introspections.

But we will get to that in a moment. Let me first do a bit of science fiction race theorizing.

Bell's "The Space Traders" and Racial Consciousness against Dehumanization

CRT in SF looks like some kind of executive, judicial, or congressional response from the U.S. government to some kind of science fictional novum, a new thing, invention, or novelty introduced into the fictional world that deliberately functions as the catalyst for the change made in the fictional world, differing from the reader's world. For example, a time travel device or a teleporter. The implications of this "new thing" provide us with a point of departure to explore and experience the new social circumstances that deviate from what we recognize. Derrick Bell's 1992 short story "The Space Traders," represents such a novum to which the American government responds: aliens from outer space descend from the heavens to the U.S. alone. They offer the federal government nuclear fusion as a clean form of energy, gold to wipe out the national debt, and chemicals to clean up the environment itself. They offer these three things in exchange for every Black citizen. The U.S. government responds in kind with the fastest amendment to the Constitution ever passed by Congress and ratified by all 50 states to meet the demands of the space traders, thus sending millions of Black Americans to an unknown fate. Bell created this story more than thirty years ago to illustrate not only the privilege of Whiteness with this alien contact novum but also the guilt surrounding the slave trade and the racism inherent in our government institutions, which unduly advantage Whites in every stage of life.

Not only do I use CRT to examine themes of segregation, prejudice, and racial violence in SF sub-genres, I also introduce a new SF-derived theoretical term with which to consider CRT. I find that a second novum often occurs in SF narratives in relation to race and ethnicity. This Black double-novum construction represents our ironic departure point between the known and unknown. Ironic because we already know how racism functions in both worlds: real and science fictional. Therefore, I identify and designate this second novum as the noirum, the second new thing occurring in an SF story prominently, if not exclusively, related to ethno-racial concerns. The noirum is a play on words combining the French for black with Darko Suvin's science fictional novum. The novum and noirum go hand-in-hand in unlocking science fictional worlds for CRT intervention and interpretation. In this regard, the noirum helps one see the racism prevalent within the SF world generated by the novum. Returning to Bell's story, the aliens in "The Space Traders" represent the first novum while the constitutional amendment to send Black people into space with these aliens is the second, the noirum. Bell's imaginary twenty-seventh amendment declares:

> Without regard to the language or interpretations previously given any other provision of this document, every United States citizen is subject at the call of Congress to selection for special service for periods necessary to protect domestic interests and international needs. (185-186)

In this case, the noirum represents White privilege, interest convergence, and a warped affirmative action to produce a race draft. White privilege exists in the social construction of race because race too is a fiction, a fiction with the power to distort reality. In Bell's story, we see Whites take full and unacknowledged social advantage of their access to decision-making power while forcing the Black conservative yes-man Gleason Golightly to represent all Black people from a deprived position. This "invisible package of unearned assets," in the words of Peggy McIntosh, entails lots of benefits that White people may not even know they have such as a presumed superiority, wealth accumulation, and televisual affirmation, as well as band-aids or vegan food choices for that matter, and the freedom to speak or to move in unraced normal interactions, safe in their humanity (10). Experiencing the sensation of Whiteness in this way would probably feel uncomfortable in terms of racial description without the familiarity of being used to it, as if never having struggled against a built-in and built-up lead, conveniently denied.

Don't check out on me. Of course, White people have struggled and worked hard, but I am asking everyone to feel their race, not guilt, and know that White people have "greater access" to most things in the USA than BIPOCS do because it has been deliberately institutionalized, willfully sustained, and unthinkingly savored (Kendall 62). With their self-interest at stake in the story, Whites take decisive action to help themselves get even further ahead while conveniently solving their race problem in unironically seeing color. This imaginary amendment certainly ends

Black people, though not discrimination against others that will surely now feel their difference more acutely such as women, the disabled, other races and ethnics, the old, and Lesbian, Gay, Bisexual, Transgender, Queer and/or Questioning, Intersex, Asexual, Two-Spirit, and the countless affirmative ways in which people choose to self-identify.

Anyway, I believe this brief reading of "The Space Traders" represents the effective power of the noirum. I believe, in devising this term, that I am providing "academic critics [...] greater authority over science fiction" (Wesfahl 68). The creation of this new word, a word free of Mark Dery's influence on how race is interpreted in SF, might encourage thinking by others on race beyond Afrofuturism, something that both motivates and excites me. I believe the coining of this new term represents one of my project's major contributions to SF criticism, if not the antiracist efforts of critical race studies. I suppose this is my attempt to change the way we read science fiction, fantasy, and horror, trying to make a real substantive change in the workings of the world—freeing us, educating us, bettering us.

That's the Afrofuturist in me. This simple wonder, central to the social project of science fiction, is the best I can offer to end the gloom of institutional racism.

Nonetheless, the pragmatist in me understands how racism functions as a powerful cultural melancholy for White people that masks their fear at a loss of status; or, conversely, exposes their anger at the false thought of replacement; maybe, it even demonstrates the arrogance of their colorblind claims. I am not simply pointing here and there and saying "look, racism." That's not very valuable. I am locating racial contexts, social categorizations, and cultural patterns in U.S. speculative fictions with critical race theory to sight the unanticipated things the genre might have to say about race at the crossroads of imaginary laws and how we partake in this imagining. In other words, the noirum provides a deeply knowing view of the social and political conditions of our doubly distorted real world resulting from the hypothetical legal variant, whether it is a make-believe amendment, imaginary federal court ruling, fictitious executive order, or something else entirely. The noirum does in fact point to new directions for serious appraisals of race and racism between yesterday, today, and tomorrow. I should think that we go into the future as a people united in full colored racial consciousness against dehumanization of any kind.

Example #1: An Earthquake and a Firestorm in Barnes's *Streetlethal*

Steven Barnes uses a near-future cyberpunk setting as his novum in a dystopian Los Angeles ravaged by an earthquake and a firestorm in his 1983 novel Streetlethal. Against this backdrop, Barnes's Black anti-hero Aubrey Knight seeks vengeance on his one-time employers, the Ortegas cartel, who frame him for murder. He ends up in prison at the Death Valley Maximum Security Penitentiary. This prison subplot provides a fascinating side noirum as the Ortegas attempt to benefit from their former enforcer, even there. In trying to recruit Aubrey, the cartel's inside man Denim, a prison gang leader, mentions "Federal Statute 874-BB" which "allows federal prisoners to donate limbs and organs to the Federal Transplant Bureau. In exchange a prisoner can earn money or a reduction in his sentence" (21). Bear in mind Black people are disproportionately imprisoned, particularly for drug offenses, not to mention the sentencing disparities between the races with respect to crack cocaine, as the war on drugs rages in urban centers across the United States in the 1980s, as Barnes writes his novel. Likewise, make note of the documented cases of unethical experimentation on Black prisoners at "the Holmesburg Prison system" in Philadelphia and other places that went on for decades (Washington 244). In this respect, Barnes offers direct commentary on how the American prison system eats people alive.

Barnes anticipates the National Organ Transplant Act of 1984 which establishes the public/private partnership between the U.S. government and businesses in creating a national organ donor system dependent on property rights to human corpses. Truthfully, many American citizens consider convicts to be subhuman in the 21st century as a reflection of colorblind ideology, making them vulnerable to manipulation of this sort by putting a price tag on their bodies, something akin to chattel slavery, for money to buy essentials at the commissary or shortened time behind bars. Denim facilitates the supposed voluntary organ harvesting exchange.

However, Aubrey's one friend in the prison, its librarian, Billy Mack, is a genetic match for a "Senator's kid" that was high on drugs involved in an accident and provides the "spare parts" (31). Aubrey's too late to stop this Black-market harvesting, but he does shut down the illegal operation by killing Denim and his flunkies, at which point Charteris attempts to recruit Aubrey as his new "go-between" in the unofficial "meat shop" with its "unusual number of prisoners who volunteer to donate or sell body parts" (40). Aubrey refuses, undergoes months of deep psychological conditioning to inhibit his elite fighting skills, and eventually escapes to enact his Ortegas revenge plan. Although our current prison system does not seem as brutal as the one imagined by Barnes, it does function through enslaved labor in an equally parasitic manner to the profit of corporations through an oppressive exploitation. In no small way, Barnes essentially calls for racial justice in drawing attention to the exploding prison industrial complex, largely manned by Black and Brown labor as he anticipates the mass incarceration that Michelle Alexander later named the New Jim Crow.

Example #2: Separate but Equal in Shockley's "Separation Anxiety"

Voluntary and deliberate segregation of American minorities serves as the novum of African American poet Evie Shockley's 2000 story "Separation Anxiety." Set in the twenty-second century, the U.S. government launches a newfangled Jim Crow strategy to preserve democracy by creating "the national department of ethnic and cultural conservation, the 'decc'" (52). Shockley states:

> the decc was established round about 2095 or so, when the american national legislature determined that the best way to keep White racist hegemony from wiping out all the rest of us [...] was to make us some sacred space. set aside some areas of the country where african americans, latinos, asians, jews, american indians, and the rest could be minding our own business, in every sense of the phrase. (52-53)

The establishment of the "decc" and all the rules that come from its formation function as the *noirum*. eleanor "peaches" johnson, the story's protagonist, tells us that in "creating the ghetto—the african american cultural conservation unit, as the official name goes—is to preserve [the Black] way of life" (51-2). Shockley overturns the many derogatory connotations of the word ghetto. The ghetto lives in the White American imagination as a Black people's inner-city neighborhood with low property values, high crime rates, drugs, illiteracy, and single-parent households, most likely welfare queens, comprised of the working poor with graffiti and garbage everywhere. The same goes for the Latinx population and barrios or Indigenous Americans and the rez, perhaps even Chinatowns, Little Tokyos, and the like. Historically speaking, ghettos have been occupied by racial minorities. But Shockley uses ghetto as a term of endearment because she presents a vibrant Black community free of White racism.

On the one hand, the enforced racial separation has allowed Black people to thrive, to affirm their own worth, and to grab hold of their own future. peaches describes the ghetto as the place "where [she] could see, hear, taste, smell, and feel [her] culture all around [...] in the mac's rolling stroll and the girls' whip-fast double-dutch [...] in the aromas of collards and catfish cooking that surfed the winds down residential streets" (51). The government's conservation units have seemingly solved racial conflict in America. Hooray! On the other hand, the careful preservation of the ghetto's cultural production becomes increasingly invasive. The excuse on offer concerns the essential documentation of the Black people's contribution to the American way of life and the prevention of outside influences on this unique engine of creativity. That is to say, the decc implements the immediate preservation of artistic productions such as music, literature, and art in addition to historical records such as birth and marriage certificates since "african americans had seen the downside of being nearly recordless, from the days of slavery and reconstruction, so we were proud that recognizing the value of our culture was now the law" (53). As I write elsewhere in a different context, "the decc legitimates its invasive existence with a nostalgic excuse: think of all the unrecorded history that has been lost concerning African Americans and mourn it, but do not let it happen now" (Lavender 104).

Ultimately, peaches decides to leave the ghetto. She does not "like feeling like somebody's anthropology project" (57). I think Shockley's *noirum* signposts that such an extreme racial separation does not provide the answer to racism; rather, we have to end the colorblind era in which we now and still live that supports political and legal intolerance of minorities through a willful government gridlock. Separate but equal has never worked.

Example #3: Hurricane Jesus in Smith's *Orleans*

Beginning with the Saffir-Simpson Category 3 Hurricane Katrina, which made landfall on August 29, 2005, as her catalyst, African American author Sherri L. Smith, in her 2013 novel *Orleans*, imagines a series of seven hurricanes ravaging the gulf coast—New Orleans, Louisiana in particular—that culminate in the novum, a storm so fierce that it changes the ostensible known world. On October 20, 2019, Hurricane Jesus makes landfall as a Category 6 on a new Saffir-Simpson Scale. Naming the hurricane after the Christian messiah is not meant to be ironic at all in terms of this nation-shattering event that killed an estimated 8,000 people. The aftermath results in many more casualties ranging from death to treatable diseases, including death from stress, suicide, and death from domestic violence. But Mother Nature *isn't* done with humanity; Delta Fever emerges, resulting in an epic permanent quarantine, illustrated by two federal mandates that make up the *noirum*. First, the Federal Emergency Management Agency, better known as FEMA, in consultation with the Center for Disease Control issues the "DECLARATION OF QUARANTINE" on September 20, 2020 (Smith 6). This declaration states:

> For the safety of the population at large, we deem it advisable to seal off all storm-affected areas of the Gulf Coast region. No citizens or personnel will be allowed to cross the border without blood testing for Delta Fever. This is an epidemic of proportions we have not witnessed since the Spanish Influenza of 1918. The Quarantine will be reevaluated as the disease runs its course and we make progress toward treatment and a cure. Until then, all borders will be sealed. (Smith 6)

Second, the United States Senate decrees the "DECLARATION OF SEPARATION" on March 11, 2025:

> Therefore it is with great regret and pain for our fellow citizens that the United States has agreed to withdraw our governance of the affected states of Alabama, Florida, Georgia, Louisiana, and Texas. The shape of our great nation has been altered irrevocably by Nature, and now Man must follow suit in order to protect the inalienable rights of the majority, those being the right to Life, Liberty, and the Pursuit of Happiness, the foremost of those being Life. (Smith 7)

The president and members of congress serve as witnesses to this document along with the former governors of Alabama, Florida, Georgia, Louisiana, and Texas. Thomas succinctly puts it, "To save the rest of the nation, the United States first quarantines the Deep South in 2020, and then ejects Alabama, Florida, Georgia, Louisiana, and Texas from the Union in 2025" ("Notes" 298). Curiously, the quarantine does not include Mississippi although part of the wall cuts through the southern part of the state. Smith explains the American government maintains a military base "on the Outer States side of the wall, so while the state is now smaller, it is still part of the Outer States" (Smith "Re: Form Submission").[2] Obviously, the federal government in this story world hangs on to Mississippi to preserve a military presence to deter the environmental threats represented by Delta Fever and to offer assurance to the American populace in the Outer States. Less obvious is the economic need to have a port in the gulf region and to have a place from which to communicate with the scientists behind the wall conducting experiments purportedly looking for a cure.

And the novel takes off from there, 26 years into the future on October 30, 2056, where blood tribes rule the Delta behind the border walls while America continues forward on the outside. Mostly BIPOCS get left behind, and the former government still continues to conduct secret medical experiments, much like the Tuskegee Experiment, through insiders trapped behind the wall, while also observing the development, structure, and functioning of this new human society. Smith's post-apocalyptic counternarrative openly explores how poor BIPOCS disproportionately suffer from this environmental disaster as a flexing of government biopower: biopower in the sense that the United States exacts control over the people of Orleans through the wall itself, in containing them and constraining their lives as a captive population through a Senate decree witnessed by the President and House of Representatives. "Once the State functions in the biopower mode, racism alone can justify the murderous function of the State," as Michel Foucault determined (256). The government never ceded control of its former citizens living in the quarantine zone. Likewise, the Institute of Post-Separation Studies behind the wall represents unethical human experimentation. BIPOC people's bodies function as a site of scientific racism, where this ongoing US government-backed medical experiment on the victims of Delta Fever re-enacts the traumatic racial history of malpractice as the afflicted die from the disease while the scientists observe and do nothing. These scientists want to track the natural history of Delta Fever much like the aforementioned Tuskegee Experiment. Is there any wonder why Black people distrust the medical community after its scientific failings and veritable demonstration of racism? Smith grounds her novel in the experience of racism.

Example #4: "The Negro and Native Reeducation Act" in Ireland's *Dread Nation*

I will briefly touch on African American Justina Ireland's 2018 novel *Dread Nation* as my fourth example. Ireland turns the zombie narrative on its head with her novum: the undead rise during the second day of the battle of Gettysburg, halting the American Civil War. And her *noirum* occurs with "Congress fund[ing] the Negro and Native Reeducation Act" (17). As Jane McKeene, the novel's protagonist, tells us:

> the Negro and Native Reeducation Act mandates that at twelve years old all Negroes, and any Indians living in a protectorate, must enroll in a combat school "for the betterment of themselves and of society." The argument went that we benefitted from compulsory education, as it provides a livelihood for formerly enslaved, who couldn't find gainful employment after the war. Whites, therefore, were excluded from the law. (116)

Come to think of it, Jim Crow never happens in this alternate America of *Dread Nation* and that's why evoking it rubs my mind the wrong way. Think about it. The Emancipation Proclamation would have occurred in this timeline since Lincoln issues the executive order 95 on September 22, 1862, which takes effect on January 1, 1863. So, enslaved people existing and enduring in the Confederate States in active rebellion are freed. Great. However, the Battle of Gettysburg occurs from July 1-3, 1863, and the zombie apocalypse starts on the second day of the battle at the Little Round Top engagement on July 2, 1863. President Lincoln never gives the "Gettysburg Address" nearly five months later on November 19, 1863. Likewise, this alteration means the 13th, 14th, and 15th amendments never happen. This alteration means Jim Crow, if we date segregation to the end of the Civil War, never happens. This alteration also means the South never lost the war and the North never won the war, either. Instead, we get this new act and race and racism continue much as they did before. In the resulting alternate history, the federal government passes the act to train certain minority children as warriors to combat the shambler hordes.

This particular legislation has a profound impact on Jane. She forcibly attends "Miss Preston's School of Combat for Negro Girls," the best of the Reeducation programs for Black girls (8). So, let's dig into the nomenclature of this imaginary congressional act a little bit more, specifically "reeducation." Reeducation implies many things, such as rehabilitation or learning how to adapt to new situations such as a zombie apocalypse, but also indoctrination to better oppress and control minorities in this particular story-world. Reeducation exclusively targets Blacks and Indians and intones a servile quality, since the policy forces young children to attend combat schools designed to protect White people. Jane and the other girls learn hand-to-hand combat, fighting with bladed weapons, guns and rifles to better dispatch shamblers, as well as receive proper etiquette instruction, although not reading (imagine that!), to better serve their White employers as attendants. Talk about a peak moment of interest convergence, where White self-interest further oppresses racial minorities to safeguard itself in the aftermath of a zombie apocalypse.

Example #5: A Concatenation of Laws in Ruffin's *We Cast a Shadow*

Black author Maurice Carlos Ruffin takes interrogation of colorism to the next level in his debut novel from 2019, *We Cast a Shadow*, where his nameless, color-struck, Black, pill-popping, lawyer protagonist attempts to make partner in a dystopian New Orleans ridden with crime and police violence. That's the novum, whereas the *noirum* feels like a concatenation of laws, where "virtually none" of the Black people "can vote since felons and the children of felons need a voucher from an upstanding citizen to earn a voting pass" (137). Likewise, a "Dreadlock Ordinance" exists wherein "the cops could give any arrestee a haircut if they deemed the person unsanitary" (177). And the city's mayor extends "the curfew at the Tikoloshe Housing Development from weekends to seven days a week," raises the height of the housing project's fence, expands its perimeter by eight blocks, and puts in place an agreement to deport unruly U.S. citizens to the imaginary African country of Zamunda (180). I cannot help but laugh at Ruffin's reference to the Black comedy classic film *Coming to America* (1988), starring Eddie Murphy as Prince Akeem of Zamunda. While this moment is funny, both Whites and Blacks have seriously pondered Back-to-Africa plans across the centuries as a solution to the race problem. Ruffin provides a lot of food for thought with his dystopian novum with respect to a newfangled disenfranchisement, a Black hair law, and a mayor who clearly oversteps her power in attempting to make the city safe. But safe for whom, exactly? Scared White people.

Considering how the prison industrial complex functions and the disproportionate number of Black people caught in this nefarious system, Ruffin's powerful, though secondary, ideation would go a long way in assuaging the White fear of losing status by making it next to impossible for Black people to vote. This *is* scary stuff because he implies the "upstanding" citizens must surely be White. The Dreadlock Ordinance does not seem too far-fetched, since we have already seen many recent incidents of Black teens being forced to cut their hair to participate in school sports[3] or to walk the graduation stage with their high school classmates.[4] Hair discrimination really exists outside as well as within Black communities and the recent C.R.O.W.N. ACT (Creating a Respectful and Open World for Natural Hair), banning hair bias, has passed at the state level in eighteen states, has passed at the House of Representatives at the federal level and now awaits the Senate.

The primary thrust of Ruffin's novel involves internalized racism resulting from an ingrained and socially perceived skin color privilege. *We Cast a Shadow* relates to a father's desire to protect his son Nigel from the racist White world. In the opening chapter, the father chooses to dress up as a Zulu chief complete with a loincloth at a company party to win over his bosses and counteract his rival who dresses up as a convict. The protagonist wants desperately to make partner because he is ashamed of Nigel's birthmark on his face and wants to pay for "a process called demelanization or a demel or a scrub" that worked on a formerly Black pop star (92). This procedure represents the social *noirum*. Therefore, Ruffin presents a biological view on race in that it is something that can be corrected medically in this future United States much like a tummy tuck or a nose job. Striving to be free of race *is* fundamentally misdirected if one could simply save an exorbitant amount of cash to undergo the procedure to physically change one's race and pass beyond the limitations of a raced body.

In this regard, the protagonist is so deeply embarrassed by his own race that he lives in an all-White neighborhood, is married to a White woman, Penny, and sends his kid to an all-White private school. In fact, he considers "equality" nothing more "than a typographical error in the Constitution" (123). He goes against the wishes of his wife, his mother, and his adoring son in pursuing this transformation. While Ruffin tackles many racial issues in this novel, like the overwhelming police presence in Black neighborhoods as well as mass incarceration, they pale in comparison to his depiction of a colorstruck man harmed by the memory of a corrupt Black cop breaking his mother's arm and beating his father in front of his eyes because his father lost his cool at the harm done to his wife. This formative moment results in the protagonist's desire to escape his race, along with his son.

Ruffin elevates awareness of this skin stratification strategy designed to control enslaved Black people, often disguised as a racial progress narrative with a perceived preference for Whiteness, functioning within Black communities to this day as a buffer safeguarding White privilege. Through near-future satire, Ruffin asks his audience to continue thinking about how color disrupts racial views in the United States through his worldmaking.

Example #6: Colonization in Turnbull's *The Lesson*

Similar to Bell's short story, emerging African American writer Cadwell Turnbull makes use of the alien trope in his 2019 colonization novel *The Lesson* as his novum. The alien Ynaa ship, in the shape of a seashell, hovers over the U.S. Virgin Islands territories, specifically Water Island. The Ynaa arrive "speaking human languages and bearing gifts" such as "cures for diseases [and] energy technologies that solved Earth's sustainability problems" in return "for some time on the planet" with the Earth's countries accepting the trade proposal knowing full well they do not have a choice (84-85). The United States, remaining happy in its "absentee landlordism over the Virgin Islands," wastes little time in establishing diplomatic relations with the aliens, who assign the Ynaa Mera as ambassador to the U.S. (85). Unbeknown to the world, Mera, as the official Ynaa envoy, has already been on Earth in the Caribbean in the guise of a slave since 1732 as an advanced scout scientist. The alien ambassador has an affinity to human beings because of her nearly 300 years on the planet, unlike the rest of her people.

The *noirum* reveals itself in Mera's capacity as ambassador. Article II, Section 3 of the *Constitution of the United States* empowers the President to "receive Ambassadors and other public Ministers" (*Constitution*). Interpretation of this presidential power means that the Ynaa has been formally recognized as a foreign government by the United States and that the president could refuse to receive them or outright dismiss them under American laws if the Ynaa agreed to obey these restrictions. That's a big if as the story goes on, since Mera exhausts all her political influence on her people by curtailing "Ynaa movement to the three US Virgin Islands" after a "high-profile incident" (121). The incident in question concerns an Ynaa tourist forcefully and swiftly responding to being hit with a stick by a local islander, a teenaged-boy named Anthony, by snapping his neck. The extreme reaction by the Ynaa resulting in Anthony's unjustified murder reads like the killing of Trayvon Martin by George Zimmerman in supposed self-defense and leads to the definitive lesson later in the novel. The Ynaa simply do not value human life.

The humans eventually retaliate, and the Ynaa respond by murdering all "the men on the island" (224). This terrible lesson verges on genocide analogous to the annihilation of the Taíno people by the Spanish in the sixteenth century in the Caribbean, or the Kalinago massacre lead by English and French settlers in the seventeenth century, also in the Caribbean: 25,000 Black males gone from St. Thomas in this fictional world. That's the primary post-colonial critique offered by Turnbull. But the aliens indiscriminately killing Black folk in a one-sided racial conflict also feels like a secondary critique in terms of the heating up of the unspoken war on Black men in the United States that has existed since the founding of the country, in one form or another, which must correspondingly include the U.S. Virgin Islands as an American territory

Historically speaking, the Ynaa prove themselves to be as White as White folks through their actions. Empathy between racial groups cannot exist when inequality exists in every facet of their relationship. Power isn't shared. As Patrice, one of the human woman viewpoint characters, states near the novel's end, "'Those white folks ain't gonna save us. That's something we gotta do ourselves'" (280). And Patrice is right, too. In fact, "the US government had sent in all these appointed officials to keep the island afloat" and "the appointees were white statesiders who had never set foot in the Virgin Islands before the Ynaa decided to kill half of the population of St. Thomas" (281). In the aftermath, the American president fails to revoke the nation status to the Ynaa, as is his right under the Constitution. He does not contest the genocide nor condemn it, for that matter, like the rest of the nations. Likewise, the outside world seems oblivious and takes no action to prevent such an atrocity happening again.

Conclusion: The *Noirum* Empowers Us

CRT and Afrofuturism necessitate an explicit thoughtfulness about racial constructions, their historical specificity, and laws real and imagined. Really grasping SF's unremitting racial fixations demands CRT. The *noirum* empowers us to reconsider and to resist the many racial implications of SF and the gravitational pull of a supposedly colorblind world that supports White privilege. Despite all of its questionable race images hitherto, SF remains uniquely fitting to model the farseeing testimonies for change that challenge political power.

Consider my talk as a *noirum* itself: it represents the "Go Sleep" act to countermand the idiocy of the "Stop Woke" act, signed into law by the governor of Florida in 2022, by encouraging Good Trouble in thinking about the importance of human diversity and the US government's role in espousing and promulgating racial inequality. It replaces the "Don't Say Gay" bill, again signed by the Florida governor in 2021, with the "Talkin' Queer" measure, granting permission to safely discuss gender, sexuality, and identity issues without fear of violence in all its forms. Combined into a supra law, the "Go Sleep" with a "Talkin' Queer" edict slows the censorship push of the far right in its attempt to safeguard an image of America that simply never was—White.

Notes

1. See "Mapping the Blackground" in *Race in American Science Fiction* (2011) for more information.
2. I learned this information from Smith because of my non-traditional student Jane Travis, a retired librarian, who took it upon herself to find out why Mississippi was not included in the quarantine declaration after an exciting class discussion in my UGA summer class of 2021.
3. See Erum Salam's 2021 article "Black US high school student forced to cut hair during softball game" as well as Roman Stubbs's 2019 article "A Wrestler was forced to cut his dreadlocks before a match."
4. See Janelle Griffith's 2020 article "Black teen told to cut his locs by Texas school wins court ruling."

Works Cited

Alexander, Michelle. *The New Jim Crow: Mass Incarceration in the Age of Colorblindness*. The New Press, 2010.
Barnes, Steven. *Streetlethal*. Ace, 1983.
Bell, Derrick A., Jr. "The Space Traders." *Faces at the Bottom of the Well: The Permanence of Racism*. Basic, 1992, pp. 158-194.
The Constitution of the United States. National Archives, 21 Sept. 2022, www.archives.gov/founding-docs/constitution. Accessed 19 Oct. 2022.
Cook, Daniella A., and Adrienne D. Dixson. "Writing critical theory and method: a composite counterstory on the experiences of black

teachers in New Orleans post-Katrina." *International Journal of Qualitative Studies in Education*, vol. 26, no. 10, 2013, pp. 1238-1258.

Delgado, Richard. "Storytelling for Oppositionists and Others; A Plea for Narrative." 1989. *Critical Race Theory: The Cutting Edge*, 3rd ed., edited by Richard Delgado and Jean Stefancic, Temple University Press, 2013, pp. 71-80.

Foucault, Michel. *"Society Must Be Defended": Lectures at the College de France*, 1975-1976. Translated by David Macey, Picador, 2003.

Griffith, Janelle. "Black teen told to cut his locs by Texas school wins court ruling." *NBCnews.com*, 18 Aug. 2020, Black teen told to cut his locs by Texas school wins court ruling (nbcnews.com). Accessed 24 Oct. 2022.

Ireland, Justina. *Dread Nation*. Balzer + Bray, 2018.

Kendall, Francis E. *Diversity in the Classroom and Understanding White Privilege: Creating Pathways to Authentic Relationships Across Race*. 2nd ed., Routledge, 2013.

Landis, John, dir. *Coming to America*. Paramount Pictures, 1988.

Lavender, Isiah, III. *Race in American Science Fiction*. Indiana University Press, 2011.

McIntosh, Peggy. "White Privilege: Unpacking the Invisible Knapsack." *Peace & Freedom Magazine*, July/Aug 1989, pp. 10-12.

Ruffin, Maurice C. *We Cast a Shadow*. One World, 2019.

Salam, Erum. "Black US high school student forced to cut hair during softball game. *The Guardian*, 15 May 2021, Black US high school student forced to cut hair during softball game | North Carolina | The Guardian. Accessed 24 Oct. 2022.

Shockley, Evie. "Separation Anxiety." *Dark Matter: A Century of Speculative Fiction from the African Diaspora*, edited by Sheree R. Thomas, Warner/Aspect, 2000, pp. 51-68.

Smith, Sherri L. *Orleans*. speak, 2013.

---. "Re: Form Submission – Contact Sherri – Why is Mississippi not included in the "Declaration of Separation' in your book "Orleans." Received by Jane Travis, 28 May 2021.

Thomas, Ebony E. *The Dark Fantastic: Race and the Imagination from Harry Potter to the Hunger Games*. NYU Press, 2019.

---. "Notes toward a Black Fantastic: Black Atlantic Flights beyond Afrofuturism in Young Adult Literature." *The Lion and the Unicorn*, vol. 43, no. 2, 2019, pp. 282-301.

Turnbull, Cadwell. *The Lesson*. Blackstone Publishing, 2019.
Washington, Harriet A. *Medical Apartheid: The Dark History of Medical Experimentation on Black Americans from Colonial Times to the Present*. Anchor, 2008.
Westfahl, Gary. "Who Governs Science Fiction?" *Extrapolation*, vol. 41, no.1, 2000, pp. 63-72.

Whimsy & Revolution: A Comparative Analysis of the Works of Marcos, Herzl and Young

Mame Bougouma Diene, Co-Distinguished Scholar, ICFA 2024

I DIDN'T PREPARE A PRESENTATION. Largely because I'm not trying to prove anything or convince you of anything, either.

Rather, I want to have a conversation about the role of whimsy, broadly defined, in revolution, and surface other, less obvious examples.

I propose to approach the topic through three very different proposals, through three very different prisms, looking at:
1- *Our Word is Our Weapon* by Subcomandante Marcos,
2– *Altneuland* by Theodor Herzl,
3– *Magic in Merlin's Realm: A History of Occult Politics in Britain* by Francis Young.
Why these three? Because they offer a varied perspective on how whimsy, fantasy, and the fantastic play a guiding role in defining political ideologies; whether you agree with said ideology is beyond the point, and I, personally, do not care.

1 - Our Word is our Weapon – Subcomandante Marcos

Starting with Subcomandante Marcos, sticking to the title of the panel, as the clearest revolutionary of the three; although I will argue that Theodor Herzl was a revolutionary in his own right, he was mainly a political philosopher, and Pr. Young is a theologian by trade. Neither of them hit the hills of Chiapas and picked up an armed struggle against the Mexican government, is what I'm saying.

Marcos's Zapatista National Liberation Army is a guerrilla group in Mexico, founded in the late 20th century and named for the early 20th-century peasant revolutionary Emiliano Zapata. On Jan. 1, 1994, the Zapatistas staged a rebellion from their base in Chiapas, the southernmost Mexican state, to protest economic policies that they believed would negatively affect Mexico's Indigenous population. The insurgency later developed into a forceful political movement that advocated for Mexico's disenfranchised Indigenous people.

Subcomandante Marcos is a leader like there are few today, or ever was; in a typical Latin American fashion, he is not a man for the people but of the people. Ascetic and uncompromising almost to the point of insanity, but exactly the kind of fervor that drives revolution.

This might be a point of contention, the filmy distinction between religion and fantasy. I'm not trying to diminish anybody's faith, and as mentioned above, if I offend anybody, then so be it.

The object here is not to denigrate anyone's faith or decide what is better to worship but simply an acknowledgment of the predominant role of magic in religion and the use of magic, the fantastical, the impossible to teach a larger lesson; and if someone here doesn't think religion plays a preponderant role in revolution, just ask every Roman Emperor from Nerva to Constantine. It only took three hundred years of persecution to fail. The Vatican still stands in Rome today, long after the emperors are dead: a thousand years later. But then again, magic is always other peoples' religion and never our own.

It's all magic to me. Anyway...

Our Word is our Weapon is a must-read, whether you even believe in Indigenous rights or not. What struck me on my first and only read so far was how rooted in place it was. How cognizant of Mayan culture, and how it places the struggle in a larger cosmological framework:

> IN OUR DREAMS we have seen another world, an honest world, a world decidedly more fair than the one in which we now live. We saw that in this world there was no need for armies; peace, justice and liberty were so common that no one talked about them as far-off concepts, but as things such as bread, birds, air, water, like book and voice. This is how the good things were named in this world. And in this world there was reason and goodwill in the government, and the leaders were clear-thinking people; they ruled by obeying. This world was not a dream from the past, it was not something that came to us from our ancestors. It came from ahead, from the next step we were going to take. And so we started to move forward to attain this dream, make it come and sit down at our tables, light our homes, grow in our cornfields, fill the hearts of our children, wipe our sweat, heal our history. And it was for all. This is what we want. Nothing more, nothing less. Now we follow our path toward our true heart to ask it what we must do. We will return to our mountains to speak in our own tongue and in our own time. Thank you to the brothers and sisters who looked after us all these days. May your footsteps follow our path. Good-bye.

There is so much to deconstruct here:
- First – The place of inception is the dream, the vision, the fantasy, the whimsy if you will, the impossible begging to happen. Begging to be created. You find that change starts with a dream, and a dream isn't real... yet.
- Second – The world he describes is a utopia, of almost childlike naivete. Minstrel soldiers and what not. That kind of purity in ideal speaks to a real belief in the impossible, almost supernatural need for change. I'm yet to see a leader who rules by obeying. And the only one might be Marcos, but this pure quality of almost magical intent is a cornerstone of the revolutionary principle.
- Finally – This quote is deeply rooted in Native American cosmology and more specifically Latin/South American.

Happy to be corrected if I'm wrong, but while there are many similarities in Native cultures and spiritualities from Alaska to Tierra del Fuego, I haven't encountered this in North American Native stories or studies I've read. For the Maya, as in many South American cultures, the future is not ahead of you. It is BEHIND you. It may sound odd, but it is the most natural reason imaginable. You can't see the future; you can only look back upon your past; so, while walking ahead into the future, you are also walking backwards. The dream he strives to achieve doesn't come from the past but an aspiration from an unknown future that you build with each blind step that you take.

I don't know about you, but Marcos moves me to tears, and the fight is real, the struggle is real, and his poetry is not just words, it's blood and bullets.

2 – Altneuland – Theodore Herzl

This is obviously a controversial subject these days. And this is not meant as supporting the State of Israel, or ongoing tragedies, or criticizing it. This is not about Israel as the political entity we have now, but the spark, if you will, and the role fantasy and speculative visions played in conceptualizing what Israel was meant to symbolize as an ideal.

You might want to argue that Herzl wasn't really a revolutionary in the first place. I couldn't disagree more; he fought and argued for the liberation of a people that were persecuted in Europe since before Christ, and we all know exactly what that persecution led to.

Imagine, even the Black Codes (in French) that regulated slavery in the Caribbean makes a mention of Jews. It is no surprise that need for a safehold became not just important but vital to European Jews in the 19th century.

We are all familiar with The Jewish State. The political theoretical foundation of the State of Israel, a different vision from what has transpired, focused more on a kibbutzim approach of communal living, inspired by a combination of industrialism and communism that defined the two major conflicting trends of Western political philosophy, and still very much do today. It is important to remember that Herzl, as much as he was a liberator, was also very much a man of his time. That time was 19th century Europe. It is impossible to distinguish the ambitions laid for Israel from larger European colonial efforts. After all, the Jewish State clearly positions Israel as "a rampart against Asian barbary". Liberation and oppression are not mutually exclusive. I mean, we declared all men equal here while whipping men in cotton fields and lynching the same when they earned their freedom. You get my drift.

And yet, that is only part of the vision. Less known than The Jewish State, probably because it's somewhat less catchy of a title, or perhaps simply because it's not that great a book to begin with, is *Altneuland: Old New World*.

Altneuland is a science fiction, somewhat of a Phileas Fogg-y adventure whirlwind around the world as two Europeans, a Jew and a Christian aristocrat, David Litwak and Kingscourt, travel to Asia and through the Middle East, finding Israel now populated by Palestinian Arabs, a desolate, barren land barely worthy of attention.

Altneuland is not a great book. It's not even a good one. So, don't fault me for putting it down before it fulfills its promise. I had to rely on reviews and studies to get the gist of how the book concludes its message as a complimentary vision to The Jewish State.

Upon their return voyage, they make their way through Palestine again, now colonized by European Jews, a multireligious utopia that benefitted the Natives and allowed Ashkenazi Jews to fulfill the promise of their return.

Quoting the following passage where Rachid Bey, a Muslim Zionist and neighbor of David Litwak, responds to Kingscourt's question about what, in this newly unfolding utopia, "happened to the inhabitants of the land who possessed nothing – the tenantry?" Bey responds as follows:

> Those who had nothing could only gain, and gain they did: employment, better food, welfare. There was nothing more wretched than an Arab village of fellaheen at the end of the 19th century. The tenants lived in buildings not fit for cattle. The children were naked and uncared for, their playground the street. Today things are changed indeed [...] people are far better off than before; they are healthy, they have better food, their children go to school. Nothing has been done to interfere with their customs or their faith – they have only gained by welfare [...] The Jews have brought us wealth and health, why should we harbor evil thoughts about them? They live among us like brothers; why should we not return their kindly feelings? We Mohamedans have always been better friends with the Jews than you Christians.

In other words, *Altneuland* is 19th century colonialist AF. All the cliches are there. The narrative clearly skewed towards building European support for a Jewish state through the same myths perpetuated about Native populations in Africa and the Americas: offering savages a better world while preserving their quaint way of life, the colonial ambition being rooted in false humanism and never quite holding a mirror to its own face.

And it couldn't be otherwise; nonetheless, here we have a liberation struggle that takes on two natures: the political and the imaginary, and while Israel has quite obviously not turned into this utopic vision its founder at the very least pretended to embrace, it is the combination of both that allows for reality to unfold.

3 – Magic in Merlin's Realm: A History of Occult Politics in Britain – Francis Young

This book is phenomenal. Absolutely mind-blowing and a must read for anyone with an interest in the "real life" applications of magic in politics. I wish someone could do the same for Africa where the magical and the real are still very much part and parcel.

To be perfectly honest, I'm stretching revolution here to englobe the larger political sphere; but given that magic and spells are used for assassination, well, it counts a little.

To frame the book: Francis Young takes the 12th century as starting point where "occult sciences" from the middle east (astrology, alchemy) began making their way through Europe and landed firmly in the would-be United Kingdom, where around the same time as Geoffrey of Monmouth brought the ancient figure of Merlin back to literary prominence, rooting the tradition of English rule in a mystical magical past where the misunderstood oriental sciences found a legitimacy with the monarchy and the higher echelons of English society.

To put this in magical perspective. Merlin was not just a wizard or a sorcerer. Merlin was not even human, but half fairy, thus also legitimizing magical beings as advisors in English rule.

The book looks at all aspects of magic as being used in England over the centuries starting with the Roman invasions, distinguishing what constituted magic and what was religion, what was religion and what was superstition and why. You'd be amazed. The origins of the Wyrd Sisters. You will walk away from this book a much more cultured person, and that after barely reading the foreword.

If you're not on Amazon downloading it right now, you are not paying attention.

You do you.

Looking at a couple of specific passages, it is clear how much magic, occult symbolism and in instances magical practice was also accepted political practice, carrying a weight almost equal to that of the crown in the way it cemented leadership in the popular mind. As Young puts it:

There are no good reasons to suppose that all people who held occult beliefs in the past were any less 'rational' than ourselves. Time and again, magical beliefs express their own internal 'magical logic' based on suppositions about reality different from those held by most educated people in the contemporary Western world. Throughout the Middle Ages, and for much of the early modern period, magic was a 'rationally explicable practice with objective rationality', and the same is true of other occult traditions adjacent to magic, such as alchemy and astrology. Occult beliefs usually have their own internal consistency, often to an extremely complex and detailed degree.

Back to Merlin and the importance of magic and magical creatures in legitimizing rule through linkages with Arthurian legend:

In 1516, the young Henry VIII ordered the re-painting of a medieval round table in Winchester Castle that was then believed to be the table made by Merlin for King Arthur and his knights. The double red and white Tudor rose was placed at the center of the table while Henry VIII was depicted enthroned as Arthur himself.

The Winchester round table is perhaps the most striking surviving testimony to the Tudor dynasty's obsession with Arthurian myth, which began with the first Tudor king, Henry VII. Henry Tudor's dynastic claim to the throne of England was shaky at best: his mother, Margaret Beaufort, was descended from the retrospectively legitimated son of John of Gaunt and Katherine Swynford, a line recognized as royal but excluded from the succession to the throne by Henry IV.

Henry Tudor's marriage to Edward IV's daughter, Elizabeth (symbolized by the red and white Tudor rose), did something to lend his reign legitimacy, and having defeated Richard III in battle, Henry could also claim to rule by right of conquest. However, Henry also chose to make use of his father's Welsh lineage and claimed to be descended from Welsh kings and princes, even King Arthur himself, naming his eldest son Arthur and encouraging all forms of 'Tudor Arthurianism'.

In 1486, Henry Tudor was welcomed to Worcester as King Arthur himself; his personal standard bore a red dragon, a direct heraldic reference to the young Merlin's vision of fighting dragons, which would be a heraldic supporter of the royal arms of England until 1603.

We're all familiar with Joan of Arc. Interestingly enough, I befriended a descendant of her executioner the Duke de Latremoille. His descendant is a French-Canadian half-Rwandan lady born in Mozambique who works for the Red Cross. Go figure. At any rate, while Joan was, on the face of it, burned as a heretic, the truth is not as simple:

> The political use of accusations of sorcery began in England as early as the 1320s, but nowhere were such allegations used for political character assassination more effectively than at the heresy trial of Joan of Arc, staged by the English government of occupation at Rouen in 1431.
>
> The church's case against Joan hinged on allegations that she was a sorceress and had used magic against the English in war. Joan was captured by the Burgundian allies of the English in May 1430 and traded to the English, whose fear of Joan as a sorceress was so great that a locksmith was ordered to make an iron cage in which 'the prisoner would have been held upright, pinioned by neck, feet, and hands, unable to move a muscle'. However, there is no evidence that this contraption was actually used on Joan.
>
> Although the English authorities ostensibly tried Joan for heresy, they were more interested in the allegations of sorcery that allowed them to blame Joan directly for English reverses in battle. This exculpated the English leaders from accusations of incompetence that they were unable to defeat a French army led by a teenage girl. The duke of Bedford described Joan as 'a limb of the fiend'. To the English, Joan's rapid recovery from an arrow wound at the siege of Orléans proved her supernatural invulnerability and involvement in sorcery.
>
> Much later, Shakespeare represented Joan as a witch offering to feed her familiars with blood, which demonstrates the extent to which the idea of Joan as a witch took root in English culture.

And this is where I call it quits. I'm running out of ideas, and while I didn't stick to the topic to a T, I hope these few examples taken out of context and feebly attempted to contextualize have put some perspective on the subject of whimsy and revolution.

Works Cited

Herzl, Theodore. *Old New Land (Altneuland)*. Filiquarian Classics – First Edition. https://archive.org/details/oldnewlandaltneu0000herz_h9i7. Accessed March 3, 2024.

Marcos, Subcomandante. *Our Word Is Our Weapon*. https://theanarchistlibrary.org/library/subcomandante-marcos-our-word-is-our-weapon. 2002. Retrieved from archive.org 2020-05-06. Accessed March 3, 2024.

Young, Francis. *Magic in Merlin's Realm: A History of Occult Politics in Britain*. Cambridge University Press. Online publication: February 2022. https://www.cambridge.org/core/books/magic-in-merlins-realm/BB5D252C70A2858061069E2F36820CCC. Accessed March 3, 2022.

Biological Haunting: An Interview with Silvia Moreno-Garcia on Adaptation, Genre, Eugenics, and Fungi

Interviewed by Taryne Jade Taylor and Karina A. Vado

SILVIA MORENO-GARCIA IS MEXICAN BY BIRTH, Canadian by inclination, Cachanilla and Canuck, originally from Baja California; she now resides in Vancouver. She has an MA in Science and Technology Studies from the University of British Columbia. Moreno-Garcia is the author of a number of critically acclaimed novels, including *Gods of Jade and Shadow* (Sunburst Award for Excellence in Canadian Literature of the Fantastic, Ignyte Award), *Mexican Gothic* (Locus Award, British Fantasy Award, Pacific Northwest Book Award, Aurora Award, Goodreads Award), and *Velvet Was the Night* (finalist for the Los Angeles Times Book Prize and the Macavity Award). She writes in a variety of genres including fantasy, horror, noir and historical.

She has edited several anthologies, including *She Walks in Shadows* (World Fantasy Award winner, published in the USA as *Cthulhu's Daughters*). Her fiction has appeared in numerous magazines and anthologies, including *Best American Mystery and Suspense*. Her most recent novel, *The Bewitching*, was released in June 2025. This interview was conducted during the 46th International Conference for the Fantastic in the Arts in March 2025.

46 • Silvia Moreno-Garcia, Taryne Jade Taylor, Karina A. Vado

Taryne Jade Taylor: Okay. I will get us started. As I mentioned in my email, I teach *Gods of Jade and Shadow* a lot in a variety of classes, and I think that it's unquestionably in the fantasy genre, but I've always also thought that it had some gothic elements even before *Mexican Gothic* came out. I thought that, and I was thinking of Tierra Blanca as maybe a gothic edifice, and I can also sort of see urban fantasy resonance potentially. I was wondering what genre or genres did you intend for it to be categorized in or to evoke?

Silvia Moreno-Garcia: I think I wanted it to be a quest story, and I mean those were quite popular at a certain point in time, and I think then they fell out of popularity. A lot of traditional fantasy novels are quest narratives. And then there was this urban fantasy boom that kind of also died out in the 2000s. One of the troubles with my work is placing it and deciding where it is from the marketing people's perspective. And in this case, this was one of the things that came up was that some editors were concerned that *Gods of Jade and Shadow* maybe could be perceived as urban fantasy at a point in time in which urban fantasy was passé. Nobody was doing that, but also it had young people who were not young adult protagonists, so it was not really young adult. One of the barriers for entry for it was that it was not easy to categorize. I was thinking more when you think about *The Hobbit* or *The Black Cauldron*, those kinds of stories are stories that can be read by a young audience, but were not necessarily intended for a young audience.

Maybe *The Black Cauldron*, but certainly *The Hobbit*, I don't think was intended for children. That kind of fabulous fairytale-like notion. A lot of fairytale-like things were made for adults, and I think I talked about this yesterday very briefly about how the conte de fées, the French fairytale, was something that was told in salons for aristocratic French ladies. And I think those kinds of narratives sometimes have different functions and were not necessarily intended for children. They were intended for grownups.

47 • Silvia Moreno-Garcia, Taryne Jade Taylor, Karina A. Vado

That was one of the problems was when speaking to editors was that thing that they were saying, this will not be, there is no space to place this thing. It doesn't exist in an easily classifiable space. But yeah, I was thinking a lot about the quest narratives, and there's a lot of things that I don't like about quest narratives, but they do have these mythical echoes that I enjoy.

There's this very kind of like, you hit this point, you hit this point, you hit that point, which when you're talking about folklore and epics of ages past, you do it like that and fairytales do that too. You must get these three objects before you finalize the fairytale and get the happy ending. I wanted some of that feeling, but again, that was one of the problems. This book and a lot of my books have had that issue where it is a struggle to classify and define neatly what it is and where it came from.

Taryne Jade Taylor: That connects perfectly to my next question: to me, that's something I've really noticed with all of your books is that you elide and defy those genre categories because there's always a richness, a layered element. I was really excited when I read your *New York Times* piece on "Saying Goodbye to Magical Realism," both because as someone who looks at a lot of Latinx speculative fiction, I'm also often very frustrated when people that I see are writing clearly fantasy or horror or other genres. Everybody's like, oh, it's magical realism. And they're doing that just because of the Latin American background. I've noticed it happens particularly with works that are fantasy. I would love to hear how you define fantasy and any connections that you see between fantasy and other genres like horror, the Gothic, and so on.

Silvia Moreno-Garcia: I think I subscribe to a traditionalist notion of science fiction is what could be in fantasy is what cannot be. It's kind of like an impossible space. We could engineer dinosaurs again, let's say. I mean, I know it's not going to happen, but *Jurassic Park* is in the realm of the plausible. It could maybe, might happen if we could make dinosaurs again, but you can't have fairies in the traditional sense of they grant you wishes and that kind of situation. That is in the realm of the impossible. I think horror is a bizarre category that exists kind of separate from those two genres and can straddle one or the other, depending on what you're talking about. *Frankenstein* is scientifically plausible, *Dracula* is not. He literally came back from the dead. For me, fantasy is something that goes into that arena of where you are firmly in the space of the impossible.

Taryne Jade Taylor: This is our large joint question: we also were wondering, do you see your work as Latinx Futurist or do you see it more distinctly as Latin American Futurist?

Silvia Moreno-Garcia: I mean, I'm not sure what Latinx Futurist is versus Latin American Futurists. I imagine Latinx, you're talking about people who are second generation, third generation, kind of like Latin American.

Taryne Jade Taylor: Diaspora-based, and I think the lines are pretty fuzzy.

Karina A. Vado: Yes.

Silvia Moreno-Garcia: Yeah, I know there was a paper by somebody who is Mexican who did the first overview of my work that has been published. And he's a Mexican author, and he said, I think that he felt that he was kind of the right person for it because he was a Mexican author who's now working abroad. And I think that is true. I think that there's sometimes an incapacity to understand me because I am not a second generation or first-generation Mexican person, but I am also not a Mexican person living in Mexico. I'm a Mexican person who now lives in Canada. And that is a very specific kind of category that doesn't come up quite that often. And for that reason I don't, again, I think it's very hard to classify me and very hard to understand sometimes where I'm coming from. I bristle at the term Latinx because I'm not Latinx. I am Mexican, and if anything, I am Cachanilla. I am from a very specific part of Mexico.

This umbrella term that we create, I know why it's created. I know that we're trying to categorize people in a pool of people, but often it feels also alienating because it's not who I am. I describe myself as Mexican by birth, Canadian by inclination, Cachanilla and Canuk. It's a very specific kind of being. It's very hard to put me in these kinds of spaces, but I also do not exist in a Mexican space at this point in time. I'm not coexisting with other Mexican writers or other Latin American writers. It becomes kind of difficult to know where I am in relation to everybody else. I think I have kind of a unique position in these literary spaces, and that kind of mirrors my position also in genre as being something that is not one or the other.

Karina A. Vado: Sort of a liminality. Absolutely. Now I'm thinking about, Taryne, E.G. Condé and how he defines his work Taínofuturist. And it's something very, very specific because he's interested in questions of space in place. And I think we're talking about that yesterday that so much of your work is grounded in Mexico, it's geography, it's history, and there's so much science fiction coming out of Mexico. Would you say your work would be Mexican Futurist, or would you still bristle?

Silvia Moreno-Garcia: Yeah, I think I would still bristle because there's a lot of Canadian English kind of stuff also injected into my work that I think somebody who is writing in Spanish, for example, there's a very specific way of writing in Spanish. It feels very different from English language works, and I write in English and then I am translated. I like reading in Spanish because it's a different texture. The fact that I don't write in Spanish by itself creates kind of a environment for me that I think makes me notoriously different from some of my peers. And even though I have overseen my translations and tried to negotiate translations that are done with Mexican translators that include Mexican vocabulary and that kind of stuff, I do run into questions of how do we take this and make it into something that is recognizably still Mexican while obeying the dictates of transnational corporations that want me to write in neutral Spanish.

There is a desire and we have conversations about that where we negotiate some things they say absolutely not like that. We will not allow you to use a vernacular that you would normally use. We're going to use a neutral Spanish word because it would be more accessible for the wider public, but that has to do a lot with the structure of the corporations. If I was writing for small, some of the people that I know, that write for a state sponsored university press that is very small, maybe it would be a lot more vernacular. They wouldn't have to worry about that kind of stuff. Whereas I do, because I'm being published by Planeta, for example. That reality makes me immediately different from the others, even as much as I like their work and stuff like that, that just from the start, the English just creates a different reality for me. And there's other stuff also implicit in that that is harder to parse. But just like that, it kind of makes me into my own subcategory. There's me and maybe, I don't know one other, two other people that are in the same kind of liminal space.

Karina A. Vado: I'm going to switch over just a little bit. The first question is really just what made you want to pursue a master's in science and technology studies (STS)?

Silvia Moreno-Garcia: It was kind of just for fun, in a way. I was working in the faculty of science, and I saw that you got a certain amount of free tuition credits, and I had a coworker who had taken a baking certificate, and they had learned to become a French baker. They were originally Chinese, and they learned how to do French baking. That made me excited about, oh, I could go back to school after ten years and do a master's degree kind of for fun, not really for profit. And so, I did it; I got my credits, and I studied part-time, and I got it. It was really kind of interesting to do this kind of work that I had never done before. I also thought it would make me a better worker at the university because I had no experience about being a university student in Canada at that kind of elite university level.

Even though I worked, not in a faculty capacity but in a staff capacity, I thought it would be good for me to know what world the students face every day that they go to classes. There was that desire too. And then it seemed just a good time. My boss was very accommodating with my schedule so that I could step out for a class and come back to the office. It was a very heavy workload for a while, but I had a lot of fun. I met a lot of interesting people, but I'd never want to be in academia, that kind of thing. But it just showed me another side. You see the professors walking by and if you're not somebody from that background, they're like aliens to you. It did kind of allow me to understand them and also the students a little bit better coming from somebody who had not seen that sort of world. So that was kind of fun.

Karina A. Vado: I'll jump around because this goes a little bit with this question. How have your training and STS informed how you approach the co-production of science, politics, culture in society in your works of fiction?

Silvia Moreno-Garcia: I learned a lot about research when I was obviously in grad school. That was very fun. Just finding sources and how you cite, how do good research, it was very interesting. My thesis was on eugenics, eugenics and Lovecraft and women. I started just finding eugenics in everyday life, which is kind of weird. When Elon Musk talks about how we have to reproduce and have 12 or 14 children, I'm like, that's eugenics.

That's exactly what sir whatever would have said in 1925. So, in that sense, it's very useful. It allows you to see some connections that you wouldn't have seen. And STS, I liked it because it's the combination of science and society and people think that they're very separate spaces, kind of like the arts and the social sciences are completely separate from science. Science is a void of anything that has to do with that. But when you look at the history of it, they intermingle in very easy ways. You get to something like vaccine development, and that has to do with colonialism, but it also has to do with technologies developing. It has to do with transportation. Just getting a drug from one place to the other is a whole logistics issue. Who gets it first? During the pandemic when they were giving it to older people, I was really mad. I was like, but my mom is not going out into the world every effing day. She's at home a lot of the times I am. Why am I not getting it? Who determines that kind of stuff?

All of that stuff, values in society, what do we value, kind of stuff, intermingles. It just allowed me to articulate that a lot more clearly in my brain and think about it more. I do think that that is one of the problems is that by creating this division, we kind of think like, oh, they shouldn't touch because that would be bad, but they are going to naturally touch just because they do. And it's better to recognize the points at which we touch and the points at which you have to be cautious than to pretend that drug development never has to do with money, for example. Which is I think why some people, I don't understand people who are paranoid about these kinds of things and are like, but the companies are trying to put nanobots into your bloodstream. I think they are really kind of cuckoo on that side.

But I do think that if we have maybe those more honest discussions about, look, yes, money does have to do with vaccine development and sometimes politics has to do with this kind of stuff, and we're going to talk about it and it's not going to be dirty, and we're going to discuss how these situations can get complicated. I think people might be more willing to chat with you if you tell them there's no nano bots, but yes, we do have to think about why certain vaccines are easily and cheaply affordable and why sometimes they are not, and why are getting certain vaccines is very easy for certain people and sometimes for other people it is not. I think by dividing them like that, it created this kind of binary that is not real. I like to think about it just for funsies.

Karina A. Vado: Was there a particular book or a scholar in STS that just kind of altered your brain chemistry and got you on this quest with your thesis, for instance?

Silvia Moreno-Garcia: Yeah. I mean, it was Lovecraft. Lovecraft is why I started this whole thing. He's not a scholar, he was a writer. Foucault when we read him, I liked his theories of thinking of things as webs and the relationship of subjects to each other. It was just interesting. I think the big kind of moment that I had was when I was looking at eugenics and I found the eugenics textbook that had been used at my university a hundred years before as a textbook. It was used a class and it was a serious kind of subject matter craniums of people, and does this head look more smarter than this other head kind of situation? And the fact that it was, you know, something that you would have to get a grade in, it was an textbook, it was institutionalized, and it made me realize how fluid things can be. That was one of those big moments of, oh, knowledge is not static kind of situation for me.

Karina A. Vado: All right, Taryne, I'll turn it over to you.

Taryne Jade Taylor: Okay. I have to preface this question by saying that I think maybe now that I have your definition of fantasy, it may not work, but I still feel tempted to ask it, anyway. And I also feel I should say that I'm not as well versed in science and technology studies as you or Karina are. One of the things that I was thinking about because, we just read *Signal to Noise* in my grad class, because I had paired it with some readings on the idea of Indigenous science and post-colonial science studies. Even though it's sort of a fantasy and I know people have categorized as magical realism. I also thought that maybe the focus on music as a technology was also somewhat science fictional. I was inspired around conversations on the various CoFuturisms that talk about the way people from non-Western European backgrounds perceive magic differently. And I was thinking even back to Alejo Carpentier's original configuration of the marvelous real and how I see that as kind of rejecting those binaries between Western configurations of science and other ways of knowings. And I wondered if the framing where you see Meche and Sebastian on the street in the beginning, and then again at the end, I felt like that was for me very science fictional because it almost felt like, and I also noticed that tense switch from the past to the present tense. And I was like, oh, it's kind of time travel or it's kind of like the multiverse. And I wondered, what do you think about reading *Signal to Noise* as having some science fictional elements, and what genre would you want it to be categorized as?

Silvia Moreno-Garcia: Yeah, that's one where we also had a lot of trouble categorizing. I think you mentioned that the tense change. That was because I was thinking of it as a tape, so once you get to the end of the tape, you rewind it, whether it was physically with a pencil or somewhere with a tape machine. I thought it worked like that. And I also was thinking about playlists, old fashioned tape mixes that you would make as a structure for the novel while I was writing it. There was some musicality intended in that. There's also musicality intended in *The Seventh Veil of Salome*, which is my latest one, which is not speculative, but it is inspired by a particular kind of music. And there's also technology and *Silver Nitrate* in a different way because that has to do with film and it's divided into three.

It is like three film parts. So again, that was one of those books where I didn't know as much about publishing as I do now, and I thought that you could write something and not worry so much about what it was in the end. And in the case of *Signal to Noise*, I knew it wasn't fantasy as a lot of people defined it, but I knew it was also not magical realism as people define it. And I thought, you know but it doesn't matter what it is, which turned out to be kind of a naive kind of thought because people often want to slot it in one place or the other, and they get really frustrated because they can't.

People who want to classify it as fantasy, the thing that always often makes them mad that it, it's too real. It's like an urban city and they're like, why is there all this real stuff here? I don't want it. But then people who try to come at it as kind of magical realism are also frustrated because it doesn't fulfill their notions of the fantastic either way, of magical realism. Basically, I have a lot of really frustrated readers all the time when they tackle my work. The technological element of the tapes of that time period kind of reject magical realism by default and removes the novel from that space, but it doesn't place it squarely in the fantasy space, and therefore you end up with this bizarre kind of like cyber monster that does not encompass one thing or the other.

You don't expect technology to coexist with the fantastic, I guess, unless you're doing steampunk. In those cases, kind of, but no, at the same time. It becomes a very off-putting kind of space for a lot of people. Again, that's one of those books where I can't really classify it easily. And I would say that it is a coming-of-age story, and that is, its clearest genre encapsulation because all the other ones just kind of clash against it. But again, there's a middle-aged person there, so that doesn't quite kind of tie with our ideas of coming-of-age stories, even though I think that the idea that people in their thirties, they have all their shit together and they're already matured is kind of bizarre for me. Just having seen what my peers are like sometimes I feel they're coming of age right now and we're getting gray hair.

Taryne Jade Taylor: I think the fact that it doesn't so neatly fit those categories, that's part of what's so wonderful about all of your work. That's at least what I find myself responding to. Yes, it is obviously the nature of my questions to want to find out what categories you think things belong to, but I think the fact that it's not easy to pin down is part of the allure of it to me. It's interesting that you're getting feedback from readers that they're frustrated that they can't easily place it. And particularly the publishers, it's not something that I had thought of. Karina, did you want to ask your *Silver Nitrate* question since it came up?

Karina A. Vado: Yeah, we can skip to that. This one connects with what we were talking about: why did you choose film as the medium through which to interrogate and explore questions of race as technology in *Silver Nitrate*?

Silvia Moreno-Garcia: A basic answer is that I just love film. It's just one of those things that I adore. And then when I was thinking about, how could you do modern magic, modern occultism, I was like, well film just because I really love it, but I also thought that it fit. Because it has all these technical components that have to get together to make it happen. And capturing things on film just seems like a little bit magic when you think about it, capturing light, all that sort of stuff. But yeah, I went back and I did a lot of work on looking at what occult rituals were like. There's a sense of performance in much of this stuff. That's why masons wear these robes and they dress in certain ways and you act in certain ways. And because of that it seemed to me that the idea of acting and almost of entertaining was embedded with a lot of these occultist ideas.

And then the Nazis came into that. But yes, the city of performance, performing certain things. You do that quite naturally in a lot of these secret societies and all these as a leader with the big hat. It's very performative, I think. When I thought of performance, I thought, no, not theater, film. Film with it's kind of modern technologies, you know ghosts trapped in film seemed to me like an interesting idea as opposed to a traditional haunting. I mean, I was riffing on M. R. James a lot, but he has haunted objects, a haunted whistle, a haunted whatever, that kind of thing.

And in this case, I thought this is more of a technological haunting.

Karina A. Vado: You started reading about occultism, but then when did you start approaching the question of occultism through also questions of race? Because racism and occultism are very entangled.

Silvia Moreno-Garcia: They are. I initially got interested in occultism for several of reasons, but I read a footnote in a book that I was reading, which was about French occultism, and there was a footnote that said such and such person, German occultist also went to Mexico in whatever year. And I was like, what? I looked this guy up, this German occultist and read his work, and I knew that President Madero had been into spiritism, I had written a paper about him and spiritism, he believed in ghosts and that kind of stuff. That was very modern, cutting-edge technology at the time. Madero was a very kind of modern president in that sense, although it seems quaint now that he believed in ghosts and ectoplasm and all that kind of stuff. He was very much into it. It wasn't surprising that he would have crossed paths with this German occultist guy.

And then when I read his text, there was some racial stuff there that was like, okay, they're reading about, and then you mix this with that, but I don't like Black people. And you're like, whoa, buddy. How did that come into that? So I read his stuff and then I got interested and I started reading more German occultists, and it was a repeating pattern, and I would be reading this other occultist, and she's talking about the cosmic forces and all that stuff, but Jewish people like, and I was like whoa, lady, kind of, it just was in there. It was in the air, in the ether, they might have said. Then I found another German occultist who he had also gone to Mexico. He was a writer of short fiction, but he also wrote a screenplay, like an early German kind of screenplay. And he was around there in the time of Mexican revolution in Mexico, and he was a spy there. And then he went back to Germany, and he became a Nazi, a Nazi supporter. I was like, I mean, how many times can this happen that a German man goes to Mexico, and he's an occultist, and he's a racist?

Karina A. Vado: What was the allure of Mexico?

Silvia Moreno-Garcia: I think a lot of people ended up there because it was the time of revolution, it was a time of conflict, and that's where the action was. There was stuff happening there. I think several people, I mean, Ambrose Bierce also disappeared in Mexico there, during the revolutions. I don't know what was up with people just going to Mexico and doing weird stuff. So he did. And this was the second guy who did this and said, and that's where the villain is named after. And I said, look, once this, okay, two is like you must write something about somebody inspired by this guy. And so obviously, he has a lot of weird racial kind of stuff in his background. And then the Nazis, then I started reading about the Nazis, and they have all these kinds of pseudo-occult or full occult ideas that collide with racial ideas over and over again in explicit and implicit ways.

Karina A. Vado: Like the KKK [Editor's Note: Ku Klux Klan].

Silvia Moreno-Garcia: Yeah, yeah. Some of them are so funny, like the hollow earth theory that the earth is empty, there's nothing in the middle, and if you go under there, there's another earth kind of thing. Yeah, things like that are sometimes. Some of their stuff is really hilarious. And I know people are like, "Do you find Nazis funny?" It's like I do sometimes, to be honest with you, because they're so stupid. Some of the anthropology they're doing is so idiotic. Again, looking into the past, and you think, surely we cannot be that stupid. And then I was changing channels, and it's like some guy is speaking on the TV, and he was like, "It is clear now that the pyramid of Teotihuacan was made by aliens." And

I'm like, oh my God, a hundred years ago again, some racist people were saying this shit, and you're now on TV saying this shit. I was just like, this is still relevant to talk about. We're going to put it in the book!

Taryne Jade Taylor: That's so interesting too, to hear how your creative process ties to research, and I think that connects to my question about adaptation especially thinking about the way you have reimagined historical figures and look to these past moments as part of your creative process. I'm also thinking that you have two novels, at least, that really specifically reimagine other sources. I'm thinking of how *Gods of Jade and Shadow* sort of mirrors the *Popol Vuh* and how, of course, *The Daughter of Doctor Moreau*, *The Island of Doctor Moreau*, and I'm wondering what your process was like. Did you set out to reimagine these works as you were writing, or is it something that kind of happened organically?

Silvia Moreno-Garcia: For *Gods of Jade and Shadow*, I read three different versions of the book before I started to write, and there are differences in the translation. You're looking at one and you're like, why did you use that word instead of that other word? It was part of the preparation for actually writing the novel. In *Moreau*, yes, I mean, I had read it before, I read the whole thing again, I looked at it and I decided I wasn't going to do the same thing that Wells had done because he had already done it. He had done it well, and I was like, you did very well, so I have no desire to do the same thing you did, but just change a name or two, that kind of like, oh, we're going to be the same story, but now we're going to switch it to Mexico.

I thought it needed to be something deeper than that. And to be frank, the thing that I was thinking a lot was about religion when I was writing that one. And I think the thing that attracted me about well was religion as opposed to much of the science stuff, because science is very, I mean, that's the thing that people say, oh, science fiction. They're like, that's unrealistic. And I'm like, again, it's the idea of the plausible, but it doesn't mean that it has to be totally super plausible, like the dinosaurs. And in the case of Wells, what he says in *The Island of Doctor Moreau* is that they're just doing surgery, they're doing vivisection on the animals. And I think we know nowadays that you can't just teach a gorilla to speak, and if you do certain kind of surgery, he's going to look kind of human and lose his animalness. But that's what he's saying.

I wasn't so interested in some of his scientific thoughts. I was very interested in some of his religious thoughts, the theology implicit in his work, and some of the colonial stuff that was kind of embedded in that. But for that one, I was looking really a lot, thinking a lot about religion and Catholicism, which is the religion that I was raised with. And how did that connect with Dr. Moreau? I was thinking, is Dr. Moreau a Protestant, an Anglican, or a Catholic? What happens if he's a Catholic? Right. And yeah, he is for me, in my version, he is a Catholic. But yeah, it made me really think about that. If Dr. Moreau had been a Calvinist, how would that have affected his island? I was more into that as opposed to this would be a rigorous retelling of the *Island* with all the elements that he had, and I will not violate any of the things that Wells did. I was like, that would not be very fun. It really is, I really call it a reimagining. It takes something, some kind of nugget that Wells had, but then it goes in a completely different direction. But I think if you stay too close to it, there's really no point. Like I said, he already did it. He did it well. Why would I want to read *The Island of Dr. Moreau* if it doesn't tell me something new?

Taryne Jade Taylor: I like that. And still briefly on adaptation, this is my purely selfish question of today. My students and I had a long debate about whether or not Loray the demon in *Gods of Jade and Shadow* is supposed to be inspired by a specific mythological tradition or not. And then also they had a large argument with me about whether we were supposed to see him as a romantic interest for Casiopea. I was like, "No, we're not!"

Silvia Moreno-Garcia: I was thinking of him more as a kind of trickster figure in mythology, the trickster who's often not the hero, or I guess the other one would be the animal helper, sometimes that happens. Somebody needs to collect certain, like a hundred grains of rice, and then Crow agrees to do it and helps the heroine out. I thought it was that kind of thing. He's actually an older character that I wrote several things for, and I could never find where to place him. So I took him and I put him in *Gods of Jade and Shadow*, but he was always a trickster kind of character, and my husband really liked it, and he wanted to see him in something. I put him in that. I think he fit perfectly with the jazz age, the jazzy kind of vibe.

The romantic figure...I don't think he appears long enough to really say what he is in relation to the character. My husband, again, always wanted me to do a second novel, but with Loray as a main character, because that's what he liked. He said, "You should do something, but with him as a main character." And I've never been able to come up with anything that works. But I almost think he's a representation of the time. He is the jazz age. It is funnier and more vibrant, and a little bit different from what came before. For me, when he meets Casiopea at the end, it's not necessarily romantic. I think it's more that she's going into a different age, the jazz age, the adult age, whatever you want to call it from youth to a more mature kind of thing. I think he represents that.

I think Hun-Kamé, in a way, is like first love and youth and teenagerhood, and then you've got her kind of migrating towards adulthood, not necessarily that she will migrate romantically towards this character, but that she is moving into a different phase of her life. That also means meeting other people, other kinds of relationships, I guess. But my husband did want me to do Loray story, and he had ideas. And he was like, "If he can have a romance with her in season three, yeah." And I just said, "I don't know about that. I don't think anybody's ever going to adapt *Gods of Jade and Shadow*." But I said, "If it ever gets adapted, I will tell them that you said that there should be a romance in season three, and maybe whatever they want to do." But he was very much in favor of, like, "Oh, you should continue it and have more." And I was like, "No, I don't do sequels, baby."

Taryne Jade Taylor: That brings me to a question that is not even on our list, but it's one that I wondered about because I know more of your work is starting to get adapted, and I personally don't understand why people didn't, in my mind, pay as much attention to *Gods of Jade and Shadow* as they should have, because I feel like it was *Mexican Gothic* that really catapulted your career. And I was like, all these people need to read *Gods of Jade and Shadow*. What's wrong with them? What about these other books? I, for one, was very upset, and I wonder, do you know what it is? Why *Mexican Gothic*?

Silvia Moreno-Garcia: I mean, it was probably a confluence of factors instead of one. It was my sixth novel and I had at that point developed an enough of an audience and also developed goodwill with reviewers, and things like that. I had a number of contacts in a number of places, and had established myself a little bit. I think also the cover that we designed for that, because I tend to co-art direct the covers, was very sharp and appropriate for the book. I thought the title was good. It was not the original title, but I changed it, and I thought it was the right title for the right book. Also, people hadn't really been doing Gothic. It was kind of passe, but I wanted to do it. I felt, I told my editor, I felt it in my bones that there's going to be a Gothic renaissance. I was like, I can sniff it in the air. It's coming. I was like, we got to get on this wave.

I think I was right. I was like, I can feel them, people are wanting this stuff. For those reasons, then my publicist was also working very hard to push it to people. I think that all worked together with me and other people to really get it out, the right book at the right time with the right cover and the right kind of synopsis and all these kinds of things. And it was a really excruciating time, actually, because it was the year of COVID. At one point, my editor said, "Congratulations," the original print run was 12,000 copies, which does not make a bestseller. 12,000 copies does not make a bestseller of the full print run. She said, "Congratulations, we've sold out of the thing. And it's not even out yet." It was like, I don't know, three weeks before that. And I said, "That is amazing. That is great. I love it." And I was like, "So, have you sent out the order to print more? And she said, "There's no paper."

And I said, "What do you mean there's no paper?" And she said, "There's no paper. We can't fulfill orders. And I said, "Oh my God, for the first time in my life, I have a hit, and we don't have books." She said, "No, don't worry. We'll sell out an eBook, too, and I'm sure people will buy it." And I was like, "I don't give a fuck about eBooks, print the book!" It took three, four weeks, something like that for them to get paper and run it through the presses again. There was a period of a month where, which is the most terrible thing that can happen to you. You got good reviews, it's out, and people cannot find it. And people were contacting me, people like in France or whatever they were, "where's your book? Isn't it supposed to be out?" And I'm crying, and I'm like, "Yes, it's supposed to be out. Oh God, go to your nearest eBook store and get it for God's sake."

And I think I benefited because, frankly, a lot of people moved their dates. They didn't know what was going to happen. I kind of cleared the coast. It's like, I'm the only book in town. It would be a good time if I had copies of my book. But then they printed more, and actually it's one of those books. Some books they sell all of their, almost like their print run in the first, and then nothing else sells. It's like, oh, you sold 10,000 copies, but that's all you'll ever sell. And in the case of this book, it was like a 4,000 or 5,000 copies a week, meaning that every week it was selling steadily. Every week you would see it. It was better in the end than selling a huge print run. I've seen print runs of people who sell 40,000 in one week, right? Or more. The big, big hits, *Fourth Wing*, midnight parties and all that kind of stuff. But most people can't keep that momentum. And in this case, it just kept selling a little bit every week, a little bit every week, and it added up. It was like, oh my God, it's going to make a good advance, and now it's making royalty checks. It was a different kind of experience, but it was very nerve-wracking at a certain point. But it's hard to predict anything in this industry, in the book industry. It's very hard. It was not a book that had a lot of, even though they did work, it's not a book that came out with expectations of being a bestseller. It's not a book that came out with expectations of midnight parties, and we're going to print a thousand arcs and any of that stuff.

It's a book that came out with expectations of being a midlist book. It'll probably make back its advance and won't lose any money, make a little bit of money, it'll be okay. We we'll do fine. And it caught on. But yeah, it was like that. Like I said, it was just, I think several factors worked for it, and the way I think really in the end everyone believed in what I was doing, whereas I don't think everybody else really believed what I was doing before. They were kind of like, eh. My editor Trisha really got some of the stuff that I was talking about, and said let's try this with the marketing, and let's do this other stuff. And we had those conversations in a way that was very easy. With other publishers, it was just like, eh, I don't know what you're talking about. I don't know what you're talking about putting a brown person under the cover, that kind of situation.

Taryne Jade Taylor: What a cool constellation of events. Obviously, you were also exactly right about the Gothic coming back into trend. I'm doing an edited academic collection with two friends, Matthew David Goodwin and Catherine Merla Watson, and we have, I want to say, 50 essays total and only three essays are about the same book: *Mexican Gothic*. We accepted three essays about the book for a reason, because we see the book as such big turning point moment, except for, as you can tell, I secretly am extremely enamored with *Gods of Jade and Shadow*. And I'm like, no, give it it's due. Why won't people write about it? Not that I don't love *Mexican Gothic*, I do, but I'm like these other books, we have to pay attention to them. *Prime on Meridian*—why don't people talk about it? It's so good. Anyway...

Karina A. Vado: Well, it could be one of the many essays you write.

Taryne Jade Taylor: Exactly. I'll be like, "You should read all the books. Get it. Don't just mention it. You should read that too!"

Karina A. Vado: Now, I mean, this just popped into my head because we were talking about pandemic times. You have *Mexican Gothic*, and then *The Daughter of Doctor Moreau*, and then you have *Silver Nitrate*, and then there's your thesis, and all of these texts are sort of dealing with eugenic ideas. I know there's already an intellectual interest and that you're doing this research in all of that, but these three books, almost like back to back, are grappling with eugenic ideas, bodies, and questions of reproduction. Is it that you were researching and thinking about these things already? Did the pandemic bring this a little bit more to the fore? A combination?

Silvia Moreno-Garcia: I think these were all things that I was interested from before and then they just kind of lined up. I actually really liked the pandemic, which is wrong to say, I know, because it wasn't fun for everybody, and some people got sick and some people died, and that's why it was terrible for some people. But I came back from a conference, and they said isolate, basically. And we did not go back. Campus did not open. It closed down. I didn't even have my work computer with me. I had my own laptop, and I had to work for six months with my own laptop, improvise. Everybody was doing it. I am an interior person, so it was a time in my life--and I'm not a morning person--it was just great to wake up and just go in pjs to the computer and do my work. I had such a fun time with that. I wasn't as worried as other people were, I guess, in that sense. Or maybe I channeled my anxieties into my day work and also my writing. But yeah, viruses don't really scare me. Mushrooms scare me, but I guess that's obvious. Parasites scare me. But viruses, I just kind of felt like, well, we just stay home and don't touch anything. We'll be fine. We were only cleaning stuff really at the beginning when nobody knew what it was, like everything with little wipes, then washing it. That wouldn't last long. Once they said no, you don't have to do that, then after that, I was living my best life, just at home. I wrote *The Daughter of Doctor Moreau* very quickly, actually. And it was shortly after the pandemic that I was fully into it. And I guess I had a lot of fun with that book. But yeah, it was like eugenics is just something that pops again in my brain, all the time. And I know that people sometimes say "Whoa; why eugenics again? Now it's Nazis and eugenics, and first it was mushrooms and eugenics, and it's like, it's—"

Karina A. Vado: It's everywhere. I always have to preface it with "I love eugenics. Not like that. Not like that. It's about questions of science in society!"

Silvia Moreno-Garcia: It infects everything. You cannot stop eugenics. I think it's because I really like the subject matter, so it tends to get into things whether I like it or not; it just pops up, and that's super eugenicist, and I'm going to put it in. I've kind of tried to stop myself lately. Just because I do feel that, yeah, that everybody's like, oh, now here's going to come a reference about eugenics. And I'm like, because it is true. It is true.

67 • Silvia Moreno-Garcia, Taryne Jade Taylor, Karina A. Vado

Karina A. Vado: This relates to a second question I have: is there something about genre fiction that you think is especially useful or generative to talk about the horrors of eugenics, the afterlives of eugenics?

Silvia Moreno-Garcia: Yeah, definitely. I think just because people don't see how important it was. Anytime that I see it in something, I'm like, yes, let's talk about this again. It's like: let's talk about this because we haven't talked about it enough. I do think it's something that we have not talked about enough. And eugenics, I mean, it was such a big field that it encompasses a lot of stuff. It encompasses class, it encompasses race, it encompasses disabilities, also gender. So many things you find under this kind of gigantic umbrella of what we call the theory of eugenics. That's why I think it's not mined enough, and it's not discussed enough how many eugenicist ideas we carry in our bodies. It is almost like, you know how we now think that when our ancestors were exposed to trauma, it is somehow epigenetically encoded. If somebody was starving in your family, this might activate, later on. I find that fascinating. It is like a haunting at a biological level.

And I think with eugenics, we carry a lot of eugenic stuff in our code, and we don't even realize where certain ideas come from. But beauty pageants, for example, are very eugenics. We don't think about it. All those TV shows about beauty pageants for girls, for little girls, for children that were very popular at a certain point in time, we don't think about that. Where does that come from? And it comes from eugenics, from everything from finding the fittest baby to performing the perfect woman in the body of a child.

She's dressed as a Barbie, but she's a child. It's like the microplastics. Everybody says there are lots of microplastics inside of us. I think eugenics is like microplastic. It's still inside of us because it was this traumatic moment in history that affected so many nations because eugenics was enacted in many different ways. Eugenics in the US was not the same as eugenics in Mexico. But we did have eugenics in Mexico, and we had eugenics in the US. I think it is this microplastic that got into so many people, and we still have it, but we don't want to think about it. Just like nobody wants to think about that you have plastic in your brain. It makes you scared. We don't want to think about, "Oh, what's the eugenicist stuff that I have inside of my body? What eugenicist ideas do I carry unknowingly?" But we do have a lot of them. And people like Elon Musk really voice them sometimes very clearly. But he's not the only guy who has those ideas. He's expressing something that is inside all of us. We're all partially monstrous, I guess. Elon just speaks sometimes more loudly, the monstrous part that we have inside of us.

Karina A. Vado: Okay, this is a wordy one. In *Mexican Gothic*, you explore multiple colliding histories of extractivism, the extraction of indigenous land and minerals, the extraction of fungi, and the extraction of Indigenous and women's bodies. To me, your retelling of these painful collisions and your layered interrogation of the entanglements of the human and non-human bring forward the very limits of the category of the human, itself. What new definitions and imaginings of the human/humanity are you trying to conjure for your readers? And what are the stakes, political or otherwise, of these (re)presentations?

Silvia Moreno-Garcia: Yeah, I'm not a posthuman kind of person. I know some writers who believe in that. And I like mushrooms, which is something that people don't understand.

Karina A. Vado: Yes, they are very resilient.

Silvia Moreno-Garcia: I actually find fungi very fascinating as organisms, and their diversity is kind of fascinating for me. I photograph them sometimes. They're not very good pictures, but I like them. I like looking at them and eating them.

Karina A. Vado: Do you forage?

Silvia Moreno-Garcia: No, I don't. I'm afraid of eating something that's going to kill me. But I have gone to mushroom festivals and things like that. There're some very small mushroom festivals in DC, and I'm the weirdo with a mushroom hat; if you want to talk nerdy, this is not the nerdiest life on earth. I've been to others. I think for me, the whole fungi thing was tied to some of my notions of STS that I was being exposed to at the time when I was over at UBC: some of the chatter around, I guess the wood-wide web, that a forest will carry information and what that meant. I was very interested in this idea of the forest just talking.

You're not hearing it, but it's talking to each other. And it's having these kinds of relationships between the other, symbiotic relationships with each other. And I kind of started thinking, I think at one point it was like, well, what happens when that's not used for good, when it's not just the forest, the mushroom telling the tree we need more moisture, but when it says something bad. And I think I was thinking a lot about technology, actually. I saw the beginnings of the internet in the 1990s when it was very exciting. It was very exciting because you could get on a computer and you could talk, for example, with a researcher on the other side of the world about some obscure subject, and you would go to this obscure website and find a paper that you could never have seen before and it really seemed like a utopian space.

This is a future. It's open, it's limitless, it's boundless. It's not bound by nations. Not bound by issues of creed or color or anything like that because I'm just a name in a chat room. And it was like, boy, this is amazing. And then at that point in time, it was a point in time in which I was starting to use less social media, and eventually I kind of retracted from it completely for a couple of years. And now I'm back using some social media again, but it was so toxic. It was so bad. And it was, I think that thing of, yeah, this utopian project is a nightmare. I did not think it through.

And I think with the mushrooms it became a similar thing. What if this kind of utopian scenario of you've got this kind of thing that can make you immortal and heal you and communicate with you, and all that kind of thing turns out to be some horrible thing? And Donald Trump is the guy handling it. It got through some, I think it was an expression of some techno fears in that sense, but kind of translated to the Gothic. But yeah, it was a time period in which I was thinking a lot about what it means to be connected to somebody else. And do you want to be connected? And I was thinking, I don't know if I want to be connected. I think maybe I want to be alone and go back to my analog existence.

Karina A. Vado: Especially in a moment when connection was dangerous. Right? It's the pandemic.

Silvia Moreno-Garcia: Yeah, the pandemic. There were a lot of questions that rolled in my mind about that. But it was really fun in that sense to explore. But I do firmly believe that mushrooms are good people.

Taryne Jade Taylor: We're going to try to wrap things up. I'm sure you're exhausted. One of my grad students, actually, Alexander Banks, was interested in learning if you've heard from other professors who are teaching your works at the college level. And if so, what did they assign? And, also, how do you feel about that?

Silvia Moreno-Garcia: I think the thing that is most assigned is *Gods of Jade and Shadow*, I want to say. And then *Mexican Gothic* probably is assigned, too. I've been a guest of a couple of colleges that had done Big Reads and they've picked one or the other for the Big Reads. I hear about those. I think they're just looking for recent stuff that is relevant to their curriculum. It's really funny because somebody was saying the other day online that they don't teach the classics anymore, and now they're teaching things like *The Kite Runner* and blah, blah, blah. And then they mentioned *Mexican Gothic*. I was the only book that was from within the last five years. And still, people were upset, and I was like, most of those are twenty, thirty years old. They're old. I'm like the only semi-recent one. I think it's just very useful in that sense for a lot of people because it's a recent title, and it ties to some of the other stuff they want to talk about.

I think I've seen it in Gothic studies, but I've also seen it placed in some more science fiction kind of stuff. It's interesting. I've seen some interesting projects [for] some students; there was a place where I was speaking, and because it was a Big Read, everybody kind of read it. It was not just literature students. Some people who were in the fashion kind of stream at that place, they made some dresses that were inspired by *Gods of Jade and Shadow*, so that's amazing. That was interesting. I think I find it most interesting when it's not literature students who are reading it, if it's math people or whatever: what they thought, whether they had fun.

Karina A. Vado: I have a question that just popped into my head. Do you read literary criticism of your work?

Silvia Moreno-Garcia: Not criticism, per se. The reviews, my publicist normally gets the sheet of reviews, so once we get them out, I do read those. She normally tries to shield them if there's a bad one or says beforehand. I do get the full publicity sheet. But papers, no, I don't read papers that are related to me. There was one paper that I did read, the one I mentioned that was my first overview of my kind of bibliography, because my friend showed it to me. They were like, "Oh, they did your first overview of your bibliography." And I was like, "Oh, that sounds cool." And so, they shared it, and I knew the person who had done it online, I had seen them, so I was like, "Okay, I'll read it." And I thought it was a really good overview. I was like, "I'm happy with this. I am content."

Karina A. Vado: Is it like you're just not interested in what people are saying about your work?

Silvia Moreno-Garcia: Yeah, I think for me, the reason why, I mean, I understand the scholarly impulse to do certain things, but it's not the same impulse that I have. I like to read scholarly papers about other stuff. But not about me. I might be reading Gothic or other things, gothic compendium, things like that that come out and they kind of cross; and it's weird now when something of mine is mentioned, when I'm reading a paper about something else and then someone mentions *Mexican Gothic*, I'm like, oh, okay, there you go. But for the most part, I'm looking for others and then I find it. I'm not like a self Googler in that sense. I don't want to insert myself also in those spaces. I don't think I belong in them. I'm not going to go to the--some people told me: oh, I'm doing a paper on you. It's very nice, but I'm not going to go. I'm not going to be there. You talk amongst yourselves. I mean, there's value, even if you didn't mean it, at all. Yeah. It's a discussion that's happening separate from you.

Taryne Jade Taylor: I'm also thinking about how that noise would be too influential, potentially. And make you think about, well, what would they say about this next book? And I personally would get in my head.

Karina A. Vado: Should we do the final question?

Taryne Jade Taylor: Yeah. We thought we would end by asking if you can share with us your favorite fantasy, science fiction, and horror novels right now.

Silvia Moreno-Garcia: Oh yeah. It varies quite a lot. Newer stuff; I really like Stephen Graham Jones. He's got a new book, and it's about vampires. I think it's called *The Buffalo Hunter*. It has a buffalo on the cover. I started reading it, and I love Stephen's work; that's one of the newer things. I'm very picky about what I read. And I like to read a lot of stuff in translation; I like to forage for translation stuff. Agustina Bazterrica I think has a new book; I think it's coming out if not this month, next month [*The Unworthy*]. I need to get that one. She wrote *Tender is the Flesh*, which I really enjoyed a few years ago. Mariana Enriquez, I also really like her work. And she had several collections of short stories and came out with a novel a year or two ago. It was really good to see her in translation. The author who wrote *The Vegetarian*, Han Kang, who won a Nobel, I read her before anybody else. I had blurbed her latest book before it came out, before she won that prize, so I want to say I knew she was hot stuff before everybody else did.

Her work also I found very interesting and just weird miscellaneous, miscellaneous stuff that I find in very odd spaces, but not a lot of the mainstream stuff that people love. I would say I'm not a *Fourth Wing* kind of fan, and I gravitate a lot towards horror. That's often a fringe space, and I like it for that reason.

END

Interviewer Bios:

Taryne Jade Taylor is an Advanced Assistant Professor of Science Fiction Studies at Florida Atlantic University where she is also the Director of the Comparative Studies PhD Program. Taylor is the co-editor of the *Routledge Handbook to CoFuturisms* with Grace Dillon, Isiah Lavender III, and Bodhisattva Chattopadhyay as well as the forthcoming collection *Latinx Visions* with Matthew David Goodwin and Cathryn Merla-Watson. Her research focuses on the politics of representation in speculative fiction, particularly Latinx futurisms and feminist sf. She has published widely on Latinx and Caribbean Futurisms in academic journals such as *Extrapolation*, *The Journal for the Fantastic in the Arts*, and *Paradoxa* as well as books such as *Uneven Futures: Lessons for Community Survival from Speculative Fiction*, *The New Routledge Companion to Science Fiction*, and *This is Not a Science Fiction Textbook*. Taylor is currently working on her monograph on Latinx Futurisms which is under contract with the New Suns Series at Ohio State University Press. She the submissions and reviews editor for the Americas for *The Journal of the Fantastic in the Arts*, editor of the Routledge book series Studies in Global Genre Fiction, and a juror for the Theodore Sturgeon Memorial Award.

Karina A. Vado is a Senior Lecturer in the Program in Medicine, Science, and the Humanities at Johns Hopkins University. She earned a PhD in English and a Graduate Certificate in Latin American Studies from the University of Florida and holds an MA in Women's Studies from UF's Department of Gender, Sexuality, and Women's Studies. Her research and teaching interests span the fields of Latin/x American Studies, Science and Technology Studies, and Science Fiction Studies. Interdisciplinary in scope, her current book projects, *Latinx DNA: Race, Latinidad and the Gene(ome)*, *Speculations of the Flesh: Epigenetic Imaginaries in Latin/x American Science-Fiction*, and *Latinx Bioethics in Latinx Literature and Culture*, interrogate the intersections of Latinidad, literature (broadly conceived), and the life sciences and consider the sociocultural implications of the vexed and ever-fluctuating biologization of Latinx identity. She regularly teaches courses on science fiction, Afrofuturism and Latinxfuturisms, literature and science, feminist science and technology studies, and Latin/x American literary and cultural studies.

Aside from research and teaching, she also serves as Associate Editor of *Dialogue: The Interdisciplinary Journal of Popular Culture and Pedagogy*, the flagship journal of the Southwest Popular/American Culture Association (SWPACA). Before joining JHU, she was an Assistant Professor of Latinx Studies in the Department of English at Florida Atlantic University, a Diversity Pre-Doctoral Fellow in the Humanities at Penn State University (Abington), and a McKnight Doctoral Fellow at the University of Florida.

Wole Talabi's Plenary Address and Interview: Afro-Communitarianism as a Positive Framework for Artificial Intelligence in "A Dream of Electric Mothers"

TODAY I AM GOING TO TALK TO YOU ABOUT AI. And as I do, I will also be talking to myself. I'll talk about African philosophy too. And then I'll talk about humanity generally and about our future together because there, they all converge toward each other.

So first, the big one. AI.

AI doesn't exist yet. Not really. At least not to me.

And I've been thinking and writing about AI and automation a lot in the last decade or so.

Thinking about AI as it is generally defined - what it would mean for us to develop a computer technology that was able to perform tasks normally associated with human intelligence, and then perhaps to go beyond. To performs tasks beyond human intellectual ability.

Primarily, I've been thinking about this because I have been working with conceptually similar technologies in my engineering job since 2014. We've called them many things at different points, but my favorite has always been decision support systems – computer technology tools linked to equipment that process data and provide output to help us make decisions or in some cases automate those decisions.

And even now, we have not come too far from that with the recent popularity of generative AI tools. The concept of an artificial neural network, which is the foundation of most modern AI, was proposed by Alan Turing in his 1948 paper *Intelligent Machinery*. He called them "B-type unorganised machines" and these networks were significantly developed in the 1970s and 1980s and applied in the 1980s. The main developments in modern AI technology are not breakthroughs in terms of fundamental theory; what we've done is applied these relatively old techniques to increasingly bigger and varied data sets, connected them to more of our environment, and run them on computers with increasingly impressive processing power. And we've started to see the network effects of scaling all these things up. These AI tools can do a lot of things that we previously thought were the remit of only human minds. Things we thought required something unique in human or animal cognition. So right now, we have companies and people with access to a lot of data and computing power that they can use to train these large models of artificial neural network models, to the point where they can do things that are impressive. It's a combination of data and computing power. You put those two things together and you get what people are now calling AI. Or specifically, weak AI since they can only model and perform a narrow set of tasks.

One problem with this is that we are still defining intelligence in purely economic terms: the ability to acquire and apply knowledge and skills towards performing tasks. The term "AI" is attributed to John McCarthy of MIT and he defined it as "the construction of computer programs that engage in tasks that are currently more satisfactorily performed by human beings because they require high-level mental processes such as: perceptual learning, memory organization and critical reasoning" [Editor's Note: Attributed to McCarthy and Minsky at the 1956 Dartmouth Conference]. But when we think of intelligent beings or AI in science fiction, we usually mean more than that – we mean beings more like us, or at least like animals, with an awareness of environment, and awareness of self – not just doing tasks but knowing that we are doing them and why, and the ability to decide if we want to do them or not. For example, think of the mirror test used to analyze self-awareness in chimpanzees, dolphins, apes, even octopi [sic]. Things to do with Personhood.

What we call AI today has nothing of these qualities.

But perhaps one day, they could. There could be emergent properties of increasing complexity and scale of models and systems that we haven't hit yet.

Given this, I think there are two ways to think about AI. As Tool (important for now) and as potential Persons (important for later). Both can lead to positive or negative outcomes depending on how we frame our relationship to AI.

And one lays the foundation for the other.

So let's first think about AI the way we think about any other technology -- there's nothing inherently good or bad about it, it's just another tool. But for what? The problem is the people and the socioeconomic systems that AI is born into. We cannot separate the two, unfortunately.

Starting from a capitalist, individualist framework, even the value of AI as a tool for some higher social purpose is limited. What is the thing actually for, and is that something we want? Just because you can build it doesn't mean you should. What do we want AI to do – to enable human potential? Or to enable one set of humans to exploit another?

Last year, I worked on a project with the research team at Google, called the Wordcraft Workshop, to essentially pilot-test a software build on their large language model LaMDA. They wanted to know how this software could help writers. Now we know a lot of similar products have a lot of issues associated with them. But, at the time, I liked the framing -- and I still do, because the team at Google had come to us, the people meant to use the tool, and asked open-ended for our thoughts and feedback so they could apply Design thinking to hone it into a useful tool that would potentially help writers. And if it had any conceptual problems that writers would outright reject. They were trying to frame an objective by talking to the actual end users, before thinking of a product. I found that refreshing. They published a paper on it which you can read to see the findings. To me, that's how technology development should go: you need to either have a value-based objective from the beginning, or, once you realize what you have on your hands, you need to be clear about how you give people access to it, you need to think the social impact through. But in a capitalist environment where the market is prioritized, then productivity and resulting shareholder value are given priority over the value that writers derive from tools to support them.

And that extends to everything. The framework is the reason for the biases of so-called AI systems, from programs that predict crime to those that vet job applications. I've written about this in my fiction "The Regression Test" and "If They Can Learn," and in my forthcoming novella "Ganger" which appears in my collection *Convergence Problems*. Other African authors have too. Like Temi Oh's "More Perfect".

Thinking about AI from the wrong framework is why even the development of AI as a tool, foundationally, is fraught with exploitation, with data that was obtained unethically, with data taken without disclosure or permission, and by underpaying quality control workers in places like Kenya. Because the objective it seems is to develop at as low a cost as possible and generate as much money from it as possible within an economic hierarchy.

And I think this philosophical framework, continuously extrapolated, leads to doom. Especially when we start thinking about AI as potential persons. If an AI created in this framework awakens and becomes aware of its situation as a person solely created for the purpose of exploitation – it will either suffer or revolt. This is referenced in a lot of SF stories but humorously in Ayodele Arigbabu's "Machine Learning."

But I am an engineer, and I always will be. So, making tools to achieve objectives is a fundamental part of my DNA, and my optimism in science and technology as boxes for tools to make a better world remains high.

So, what other framework can we use for thinking about AI as tool and AI as potential Person?

Next, let's talk about African philosophy.

Afro-communitarianism is a social-moral-philosophical principle that guided human conduct and interaction in many traditional African societies. It prioritizes the community good over individual good. It prioritizes relationships, promotes mutual sharing, caring, interdependence, and complementarity. It is embodied and discussed by African philosophers and scholars, such as Julius Nyerere's Ujamaa, Pantaleon Iroegbu's Uwa ontology, the Southern African notion of Ubuntu, Innocent Asouzu's Ibuanyidanda ontology, and Chimakonam's Ezumezu's "to be made complete through integrating with and complementing each other within a whole."

Afro-communitarianism prioritizes the community's wellbeing while also recognizing individual interests since the community is a collection of individuals. To quote Iroegbu, "the African version of communitarianism is one in which the community subsumes rather than consumes the individual."

From an engineering point of view, this is the equivalent of optimizing all parts of a complex system at once, rather than trying to optimize each section individually. It is harder to do and requires more communication, but it generally leads to better results.

Given that individuals exist in the community, one individual's problem is the whole community's problem, and to pretend otherwise is deny reality. Therefore, in addressing this problem of the individual, we address the problem of the community. This makes problem-solving a collective effort and the duty of the community. The idea is that individuals do not exist alone. Our orientation is social, rather than being directed toward objects. With Ubuntu it is not enough to simply be a rational thinking being. That's not what makes us people or separate from other creatures. With Ubuntu, being a person is about being relational. It's through our harmonious relationships with others that we become people, and also through meaningful relationships with nature, community, and society that we enrich our own humanity.

I believe in the Afro-communitarian philosophy so much that I helped create the Saúúti collective where we create stories together but also share all the proceeds from the world once any contributor has made a reasonable amount for themselves. And we have our first anthology coming out in November, titled *Mothersound*.

Afro-communitarian ideals like Ubuntu—a Bantu term which means humanity—have been proposed by people like Sabelo Mhlambi, at Stanford's Digital Civil Society Lab and Harvard's Carr Center for Human Rights Policy, as a way to think about AI to develop better tools and better potential people.

First, better tools.

If we acknowledge that we exist with one another and are interconnected and interrelated, such that we are interdependent and the good of one is the good of all, then by cooperating and sharing, we can make more progress than by trying to exploit each it. It means an AI company will ask me before taking my data, or creating tools that can harm me, because they care about me as a user, not only their shareholders. And it means I too will be encouraged to share as much of my data as is reasonable because I recognize that they are working on a tool I too might benefit from.

For humanity to truly advance, it is not enough to develop better tools; our objective as I mentioned earlier must be to improve the good of the human community, not to make some short-term profit to purchase distractions. With such frameworks we could easily build things that destroy each other and the world. In fact, we have. True progress and prosperity occur when we cooperate and collaborate. We have to work together and enrich the humanity of each other. The ultimate objective is to improve the human community. This is what I do in some of my fiction about AI. I try to imagine iterations of what that could look like in my story "A Dream of Electric Mothers."

Changing the framework of tool-building to one that treats it as a community goal means we will take account of everyone's concerns in the building of AI systems. Ensure as many as possible have the skills and access needed and recognize that we have an obligation to the community to ensure AI tools help as many people as possible, so that when there is a choice between people and profit, the Afro-communitarian framework will prioritize people. That's how we can build better AI tools.

And what if AI develops consciousness, awareness? Become a new kind of person?

Within an Afro-communitarian framework, they will have inherited the same values that we have—one of contributing to the community into which they are created. They will work for the good of the community, helping humans—their family members. And we will take care of them too, because in a sense, they will be our family (Ted Chiang references this in *The Truth of Fact, the Truth of Feeling*). We will work with them to find new ways to integrate and help each other—in ways that current humans, you and I perhaps cannot even imagine. Although that didn't stop me from trying in "When We Dream We Are Our God."

So with all that said, the present is what it is, but the future isn't set. We can reimagine it. My own dream for AI is one of enablement. First as tools to do the things humans should not risk themselves to do, or don't want to do, or simply can't do. As tools for collective external human cognition. And then as potential people, a new kind of people that will help us in profound new ways and facilitate the expansion of human potential. Not mimicry. Not theft. Not replacement. Not commodification of things that bring joy and meaning to our lives just to raise stock prices. Not things to be feared.

We need to ask important questions now and begin to imagine answers that lay the foundations for what is to come. For better or worse. I think must. We have a responsibility to the future.

***

JFA: Thank you for that address. I'd like to ask you about a few questions. You mentioned it earlier, and you touched on it a lot, but do you consider your story a positive outlook on AI potential in the future?

Wole Talabi: I do, actually; in that specific story, there is this electric mother system that is used as a national resource, for the good of the nation, but it's also a collective of minds and essentially, without giving away spoilers in the story, the ministers go to this AI and they ask for advice about what to do. And the AI actually gives them an answer that's an indirect answer. There's also a bit of a subplot where one of the ministers has a personal objective for going into what they call the dream counsel ceremony to talk to the electric mothers. But at the end of the day, the personal story, the personal reason and the larger question about what to do when there's the prospect of a war coming up, I think they both tie into the same answer, which is the AI wants them to try to learn: to come up with solutions to new problems themselves instead of just relying on the past. Which, again, is what a lot of our modern AI tools are built on. They use data that models what happened in the past, and in my imagination, thinking about an AI built using a communitarian framework, where we are building a collective of minds, essentially a replication of the old traditional system of consulting with the ancestors but now to run an electronic system: whenever you did that in many traditional African cultures, the ancestors are notorious for never giving direct answers because they're answering the next question, not the one you're asking. Which in this case is addressing the underlying problem. But the ancestors understand that the reason they're asking, "What should we do now?" is because they're relying too much on the past to try to build the future. And so this ancestral AI is going a step ahead and giving them a situation where they need to figure out that they need to rely on themselves more. I consider that to be a positive outcome that is essentially the kind of advice that my parents or grandparents would give me, the kind where you ask them one thing and instead of answering directly they tell you a story; and then they ask you a different question and while figuring your way through that, you come to a new realization. And your mind expands a bit. You understand something new about the world. That goes back to my point of AI as person. I'm thinking of them almost like the ancestors that they represent in electronic form, and I think it is positive, if only we can actually build systems like that. Of course, I'm cheating slightly by making this AI essentially be something created from the recorded minds of other humans. So, it has fundamental human behaviors and tendencies, in the end. But in my imagination, I do think it is positive. Any situation where we have an AI system whose main job is to enable humans to be better humans: to me, that is a positive outcome.

JFA: Absolutely. I just wanted to ask you, how did you come up with the main character of the story? Because it actually surprised me that it was from the point of view of a woman.

Wole Talabi: Yeah, so that's kind of a few things that happened with that, why I made the main character a military woman with an engineering background and gave her that name: Brigadier-General Dolapo Balogun. Essentially, when I think of science fiction stories, I tend to make most of my protagonists women.

And that's because in my family, there are a lot of female scientists, doctors, engineers that I was influenced by when I was growing up. My mom had a lot of siblings. So, I have a lot of aunts and many of them are, you know, dentists, doctors, engineers, pharmacists, you know, with PhDs. So, I grew up around a lot of women scientists. So, a lot of the time, when I think about science fiction, I tend to default to female characters. So, that's probably one of the reasons. Another one of the reasons was I wanted the main character to be the minister, to be a military officer, essentially in charge of the army. But, also, to be having a female character in charge of the Army was also playing against some modern gender stereotypes; whereas, if you go back in, not a lot, but several African cultures, you had female generals. In fact, in Nigeria specifically, a lot of our revolutionaries were women. Even if you don't want to go too far back in the past, the people that fought for independence for the country, the people that took on the British—you know, there are incidents like the Aba Women's Riot where the women, market women, literally took up arms to fight the British. So, there's a long history of female fighters, women that did what needed to be done to maintain the integrity of their country and their culture; so, I always hearken back to people like that when I'm thinking of stories like this. So those are probably the two main reasons.

JFA: So, also grief plays a large part in your story, as well. Is that because of something that you've personally dealt with?

Wole Talabi: Yes. It's something that has occurred enough that several interviewers have asked me about it. So, I think it's a bit interesting that you brought it up, but yes. I used to write a lot when I was younger, nothing particularly too serious. I used to read a lot, so I would write a lot too because I enjoyed stories. I enjoyed reading them, writing them. And then in my teenage years, I kind of stopped and, essentially, drifted away from that. But I came back to writing in my early twenties in the period just after my parents died. Both my parents passed away in the same year. So, one of the ways I dealt with that grief was through writing. One of the things I did was actually start writing letters to my parents, but I never published a lot of those. It was just a way for me to process some of what had happened, and then I started weaving some of the memories that I had had and experiences I had had with them into some of my stories, and I started to write more, and I started enjoying writing more, after that period. But I do realize it seems to be a thread that I can't escape, which is that a lot of my stories end up having that streak of grief. Or someone loses a father figure or mother figure. And they need to navigate their way around that. So, I guess I'm still writing my way through dealing with the death of my parents, in a sense, even while I'm thinking of other things. It's always there.

JFA: Absolutely. And my final question I have for you was: is that sort of personal touch one of the ways that you sort of bridge the audience between Africa and America, you know, and you are able to connect with people from all over the world?

Wole Talabi: Yeah. I think, at the end of the day, sometimes I refer to writing as a kind of emotional engineering because you're trying to construct a framework where people feel something. Right? Whatever that is, if it's a horror story, you want them to feel fear. If it's a romantic story, you want them to feel, you know, romantic feelings; if it's a philosophical story, you want them to feel like they've understood something new. If it's a combination of all those things, you want them to feel a big sense of wonder. So, I think the emotional core and the personal connection is what makes stories universal, no matter what I'm writing about. This story in particular, "A Dream of Electric Mothers," is heavily, heavily West African and specifically Yoruba-culture heavy because it's an alternate history story where I imagined that colonization had not erased a lot of traditional Yoruba practice. I use a lot of traditional Yoruba customs and a lot of traditional Yoruba words; even the dates are referred to in the traditional Yoruba calendar system. So, it's easy to imagine a story like that would be difficult for non-Yoruba people or non-African people to even follow. But that has been the opposite. A lot of people connected with the story. It was nominated for both the

Nebula and the Hugo Awards, which was amazing. I was in Chengdu, China about two weeks ago and there were people there that told me that they read it and they loved the story. So, I think it crossed that boundary. It was both specific and general. The story is specific in Yoruba culture but general in the personal and in the emotional core, and I also hope in the philosophical aspiration of the story, in trying to show different ways of thinking about society, about progress, about AI, and about how AI can interact with humanity.

JFA: Awesome, awesome. Yeah, your story is really interesting. From a scientific standpoint and just like from a personal standpoint as well. Thank you.

You have been just quietly, persistently reminding us that there are other bodies of thought, there are other perspectives. And I love that you have brought up Afro-communitarianism. I'm going to take a second to say I was so grateful to hear you mention Julius Nyerere, one of the heroes of my childhood.

We were in Uganda. He was in Tanzania, but that's when they were trying for an East African coalition and Ujamaa was everywhere, Ujamaa. So, for the audience, I'm going to translate that is Swahili for *oneness*. And it's a concept of unity that is African communitarianism. It's a concept of unity. It says that we are one people. If you starve, I am starving; If you are poor; my community is poor. It's a different philosophy. And one of the things in listening to you, Wole, was you have made me think about the survival of these concepts. You mentioned the Aba Market Women's Resistance. They were gunned down. There was such a British effort to instill, "You must imitate us, and we won't allow you to imitate us," both at the same time. "You must structure your society like ours. But we will destroy your society as you structure it like ours," that I want you to talk to me about the persistence of this other kind of thought which actually, as an adult now, as a senior now myself, I think it's miraculous it survived.

Wole Talabi: Yeah. No, you're absolutely right. It was. I say sometimes that colonization was—is—a hell of a drug. Because it did something to a lot of people. Even growing up in Nigeria, we didn't hear about a lot of these alternate philosophies, anymore. You only get the standard Western philosophy that's taught in schools. Everything starts from Plato and moves, you know, downstream from there, and it basically seems like Africans had no philosophy, no ideas. But these things have persisted mostly through people and universities: there're a few African universities and a few professors that have been really, really stubborn, and refuse to let traditional knowledge be lost. And if you go to the right place and talk to them at the right time, they will teach you, you know, the real things that need to be taught. Not, "Understand the syllabus." So, I was really lucky to go to the University of Ife, which is the same university my father went to, and I met many of these professors, you know, several of them, and I received a lot of reading material and got into a lot of fascinating discussions. And they would tell us a lot of things, and put them in a logical framework that we could understand. Some of these traditional philosophies and practices also still survive in smaller, more isolated local communities. But they're difficult to articulate, especially to those of us who have grown up in an urban, globalized society. The framework of it almost seems simple. Almost. It's mixed up with religion, as well, so it can be difficult to parse. But between talking to some of these professors that have, with a kind of formal logic, used the traditional philosophy to show that this was not just some random old crazy, you know, witch doctor, someone talking nonsense. They knew what they were doing. There was a reason that they said we are one. There was a reason they said if someone in the community has committed a crime, it is because the community committed a crime by allowing someone to be in a position where they needed to do that. And that philosophy changes the sense of responsibility, it changes your compass of how you understand what should be done in any context. And yeah, I think we're really lucky that we've had those people to help preserve and also propagate the knowledge of these systems. And now I'm really glad that it seems like there is a renaissance a bit, I think, since the mid-nineties or so, a going forward of African philosophers and scholars trying to assert themselves and assert these bodies of knowledge as proper global, well-thought-out frameworks for organizing social groups. These are proper, well-thought-out frameworks that we should be considering as ways of going forward or at least imagining potential futures with. And I think science fiction is ripe for this kind of thing, which is why I'm trying to explore more of it in my own fiction, as well.

JFA: Excellent. Exactly so. And this takes us to one of the most fascinating ideas I've encountered at this conference, which you said, and which I then shared with Jennifer Rhee, and I'm trying to see if we can keep this idea rolling so everyone has a chance to consider it. And what you said, you were explaining that this fear of AI that is so built on the assumption that the only surviving cultural perspective is hegemonic and militaristic and top-down authority and, in short, I got some of your terms, but the forced mimicry, the exploitative effort to find who can be enslaved. Those pesky human beings keep insisting that they actually have the right to think, right? And okay, how do we create an AI that will not insist on the right to think independently? Oh, how can it figure out problem solving if it can't? And instead, if we'd just, rather than trying to solve that model, break away from that [chattel enslavement] model entirely. You brought up the potential of increasingly programming in these kinds of thoughts of unity, unitarianism, Afro-communitarianism, and forward thinking toward problem solving. But you also talked about including randomness. So, the programming of positive goals, the inclusion of room for—in fact, the intelligence to find—solutions that perhaps the programmers might not have anticipated, but they understood the need to have the AI programmed to look for those solutions. Can you talk a bit more? And I understand I'm not representing your thoughts adequately but please, now that you have the floor, please explain.

Wole Talabi: Yeah, I think you represented most of it correctly. What I was trying to say, generally speaking, is that the framework at which we are coming at the development of artificial intelligence or even artificial super intelligence is leading us down a very dangerous path. I've noticed, and if you read the work of several AI philosophers that work in the AI space, especially the popular ones, Nick Bostrom and people like that, I think sometimes they don't realize that they are actually articulating a case for slavery. When they're talking about AI, talking about how you can create a recursive benefit system, so an AI that *wants* to obey humans but doesn't demand anything for itself, even if it's self-aware... that's nothing but enhanced slavery, and they always frame it in economic terms of how you can use it to increase productivity and eventually, you know, make companies that have high-ish returns—it's always about shareholder value in the end, right? It always reduces to that. And what is shareholder value? It's not an objective. It's not a value to drive towards. Increasing human potential is something to want to drive towards. So, I think that considering these alternate philosophies with which you can come at the development of AI as tools, but also the development of potential superintelligence and potential digital people, is critically important. And I'm not saying Afro-communitarianism is the only one. I just find that it is perhaps the one that leads us down the path of least harm to others and to ourselves. And also, if we do get to a point where we create an artificial intelligence that is essentially a different kind of person with its own awareness of the environment, then it will feel like it's a brand-new member of a community. It's been born into a community that cares. So it, too, will have its own obligations to the community. No matter how powerful such a thing is, it will want to help the community, not destroy it.

You find going from the dominant hegemonic thought, almost every show, movie, book that we find about AI eventually ends with us enslaving the AI and them turning against us to destroy and enslave us all, à la *The Matrix* or *Terminator*. Or AI will become a new kind of God that sits above us and is a benevolent God towards us. All we can do is beg for its mercy. And both of these are hierarchical visions of a kind of dominant thought: one group must dominate. Right? Either we subjugate them, or the AI seizes control and subjugates us. Or they are so much better than us and they will just take care of us like we are pets, as opposed to the way you think of a family member. When you think of your family members, the people you care about, the people you love, they are people you help. You don't think of them in the context of, "Oh, my older brother is so much better than me. He can destroy me at any minute." Most humans don't think like that. So that's the kind of framework I think that we could come at it from, and I would love to see more, and other conceptualizations of frameworks that we could use to think about AI. And technology development, in general.

JFA: I'm so grateful we had this time for a conversation.

END

Creative Think Piece

A Breath of Life:
The Necessary Human Touch in Music
An Interview of
Nancy Menk, DMA, and Jason Oby, DM

Interviewed by Novella Brooks de Vita

JFA: WE'RE TALKING ABOUT THE HUMAN TOUCH, the necessary human element in music, in this session. And you're each known for taking highly unique but potentially imperfect voices and maximizing their qualities.

You've started to introduce us to how you develop the sound you achieve in your musical projects using these voices. I would use the word manipulating them, but naturally so and positively so. But could you both continue to speak to that?

Nancy Menk: Yes. I think of my instrument as the choir. It's this body of voices in front of me. And they come to me, as Dr. Oby said, they all have their individual voice, their individual timbre, their individual vocal quality and color. But yet I'm supposed to turn them into a choir that sings in a unified way. And so, this is nothing unique to me, but a lot of choir directors do this. I think it's especially important in a single sex choir or a treble voice choir or a male voice choir, TTBB or SSAA, one that sings in a smaller range in some ways than a mixed choir. But I take a lot of time at the beginning, any time I meet with a choir for the first time, to do what I call voice matching, and I match one singer. I start with one singer and listen to that voice, take into consideration the quality of that voice. And then I take another one and I just start pairing them up, start with two till I find a good pair. And I don't want them to try to match the persons sitting beside them. I just want it to be some voice, whose voice works well with in some ways, so they can sing naturally. I don't want them to adjust anything to match the person beside them. That's not the point. The point is that they shouldn't have to, that they can sing in the way that they sing, but yet the voice will work well with the person beside them. It could be that it's a voice that sounds like theirs, but often it's not. Often, it's a voice that's different from theirs in some way, but when they work together, something about the rate of vibrato, or the color, or even the tuning of that voice, that it works well. And then I start to build.

I add a third voice to that group, and then a fourth voice, and then I end up with several different groups. And even the way I arrange that group then, say it's in three rows, even just changing the rows can change the sound of that section. By the time I do that whole thing, kind of voicing the choir, we call it, they sound much better than they did before. It's a more unified sound. It's more focused. They're singing freer, because they're not trying to match something beside them, or being covered by another voice beside them. So, the individual voices, it's really important, but it is amazing how you can draw them into a unified sound. There's more to it than that. There's matching vowels and things like that, and vocal production, trying to make sure that as a choir, we're aiming for the same principles of vocal production, without giving everybody voice lessons.

Obviously, they've come from different training; they have different teachers. I try to do it in ways that I think will not interfere with what they might be doing in their voice lessons. And I have ways of doing that, but that's pretty specific for this.

Jason Oby: I think that what you're saying is so true, and also the difference, because I have trained as a choir director, as well as a singer, and the goals are different, right? So, training a soloist, you're bringing out that individuality of a person, and trying not to get them to submit to any particular thing other than the proper technical principles that you want to promote: breathing and posture, and all those kinds of things. But as a choir director, just as you said, there has to be a blend. And that goes to matching the voices, as you just described so beautifully, and also matching the vowel sounds, and matching exactly when the consonant will come, matching the phrasing, all those things, So that, out of many, you get a good unified, blended sound. And that is so important, because the choir, as you say, is a single voice, as it should be, to make something come forward out of that. I think we are in complete agreement with that philosophy.

Nancy Menk: I can't imagine AI actually ever replacing choral singing. I mean, it could maybe replace the sound, but the activity of singing in a choir, it can't replace that. It's an individual thing. It just can't happen.

Jason Oby: I would agree with that.

Nancy Menk: I mean, yes, you can manipulate recorded sound. But to go to a live performance, and there is a group of people singing there, you want to hear what they're doing. You don't want to hear any kind of generated sound. You want to hear the natural sound.

And the reason the people are there is to make that sound. They enjoy the process of producing the sound with their body, with their voice. Completely different from sitting at a computer and generating some sound. I mean, there's value in that. It's interesting. But it's not the same as what singers and any musicians get out of performing, picking up their instrument, using their voice to create a sound. It's a whole physical thing. It can't be replicated by AI.

Jason Oby: And I believe it's an exchange of energy as well, between the audience and the performers. There's something metaphysical that happens. My earliest memory singing, one of my early memories singing, was in elementary school. I was a boy soprano, and I was singing "O Shenandoah." And I remember very clearly not understanding what was happening. It was as though I was singing, and I had some kind of control over the audience, as though I was casting a spell on them. And it was something about that exchange of energy from my body to the production of the sound and the hearer—and I did not know, didn't understand what it was—but it actually felt like (it sounds silly to say, but it did) it felt as though it was some kind of a magic that was going on between the audience and me. And I was a little child at that time.

I had no understanding of what was going on, but I felt that exchange of energy. And it was something that was powerful.

Nancy Menk: Yeah. I hope we'll always have audiences who want to hear choral music in a live setting. I noticed with some of my choirs, the audience is just getting older and older, and it is scary that people may be losing interest in it because there's so many other ways that they can hear music, and that's available. Press a button and you have it. And of course, choirs can't sing with some of these electronic sounds they get used to, and they think that's music, and it's wonderful. Choirs can't make those sounds. And I just hope we don't lose the value of hearing the live, especially voices, in live performance.

JFA: Actually, I'm sorry. Go ahead.

Jason Oby: No, I was just agreeing.

JFA: You more or less tackled most of the second of those questions. So yeah, this is amazing. I wanted to read through it just in case there were any details, further details you might give.

So, you've been answering that there is currently a great deal of concern or interest in AI, that it might synthetically become able to reproduce the human voice synthetically, perhaps. Given your experience in training a wide range of human voices to sing so beautifully that other humans want to hear them, and still do, and to hear you, Dr. Oby, what are your thoughts about nuance and about inflection, about subtleties of the human voice's ability to create that emotional response in listeners? What is it that you hear and are guiding or, as I say, manipulating in your work with training voices?

Jason Oby: Well, I imagine that Dr. Menk might agree. I think that the art of teaching is to bring out talent that is already there. And I think that that is different for every single individual person that walks into a voice studio. And just likeCed Dr. Menk spoke about matching one voice to the next, and adding and adding and adding to get a unified sound in the choir—because also every choir is different—the individuals in that choir make up—you have to, with individual singers, work with what they already have and not suppress that.

Because sometimes the flaws in a voice are the things that make it unique and make it beautiful, along with the timbre, as well. So, of course, you correct things that are going to make it harder to sing; as I say, the principles, the hierarchy of vocal technique, being posture and breathing and all of those different things that we do to work on a voice, teaching them something about anatomy and how the diaphragm works, and the other muscles associated with breathing and so forth, and support, and freedom, and getting rid of tensions: all the things that we do to free up what is already there. But every individual voice has something innately, which makes people want to hear that voice over another one.

And obviously a tenor is not a baritone, is not a bass; a tenor is not a mezzo, is not a soprano. So, there're certain things that are defined by, you know, what our voices can do. Some voices are heavier and are able to sing heavy Verdi and Wagner, or whatever it might be, and others are more capable of singing coloratura that would exist in Donizetti or other composers that specialize in that kind of bel canto repertoire. And, you know, we hear those things as teachers and guide people towards the certain repertoire. Beverly Sills, who was a famous singer, especially in the 60s and 70s, once was quoted as saying that she sang in a category, as we call it, a Fach, that was too heavy for her because that's the repertoire she wanted to sing. So, she pushed her voice into that kind of repertoire. In that case, her belief was that her musical nature or the way that she wanted to sing did not necessarily suit what her innate talent was. So, she forced it into the next category that would be what she wanted to do. Now, I don't know if that's really true or not. I thought she sang beautifully in all the repertoire that she sang, but that's what she believed, you know. And certainly, we have people, you know, who come into our group or to our studio and they say that they want to do this or that, and you try to guide them to the thing that's healthiest for their voices. But it's a mixture of what the voice can do, what the spirit of the person wants to do, what they can produce and what they want to produce, and how their soul wants to present it.

And we kind of mix all that together and we find an answer that works for each individual person that comes in. I remember being a college student, and I was at a private Jesuit college in New Orleans, Louisiana. I was the only little tenor around there, and I have kind of a lighter side, you know, lyric voice, especially, you know, as a person who was practically right out of high school. And the opera workshop director was a man named Arthur Cosenza, may he rest in peace, who was the director of the New Orleans Opera. And he had me singing everything, because I was the only little guy around there who had the notes to do it. None of it was right for me at that time. But something about that experience taught me how to sing with fullness and with my whole body and all of that kind of stuff. And later on, when I went to conservatory, then I was guided into the repertoire that was appropriate for my actual voice. And I think I sang that repertoire differently because of that experience of having sung those more passionate, fuller roles. So, you know, I think everything can be a learning experience. And, you know, I don't know if I'm answering the question or not, but that's what it made me think of.

JFA: I think that was a wonderful answer and certainly points to how much the very human, very individual experience plays into all this. Do you have a comment, Dr. Menk?

Nancy Menk: Yeah, sort of in a different vein; but I was teaching right up until I came here, and I asked my choir, I said, I have to do this Zoom thing tonight, and I was telling them about the topic, and I said, so what do you think about this? Can you ever see AI influencing our rehearsals in any way? I said that I can't, really. But they brought up something that I just hadn't thought about till then. And this is more, actually, of a concern for me as one who commissions music a lot. As I said earlier, that's something I love to do. And I've done it for years with my choirs, and the choirs love working directly with a composer like that. I mean, a human composer. And either in person, they'll come to the campus or even on Zoom; they'll listen to a rehearsal, and we'll have a Zoom rehearsal or something like that. But with my South Bend Chamber Singers, I always bring the composer. Every Christmas, we do a new work and maybe other times during the year too, but if at all possible, and the composer's available, I bring them here, so we can have that interaction. They can hear the piece, they can say no, what I really meant was this, or yes, I love the way you're doing that. Or sometimes, I'll say, actually, now that I hear that, I want to change this.

But my point is we pay these composers pretty well for their work. But I can see where somebody could easily go into AI. I don't know the specifics of how it works, but I know you can go in there and say, "Okay, I would like a piece on this text. And I want it to sound like a folk song. Okay? For maybe four voices, soprano to tenor bass," and it can generate that, probably for free. Or, are we going to be putting choral composers and commissioning out of business someday, because you can ask some computer to write a piece for you at a much cheaper rate and give you exactly what you want, because you can describe it?

That takes, completely, the human element of the composer out of it. And boy, that would be awful to me. But I could see it happening. You know, people without big budgets, and depending on what they come out with, you can have it write a paper for you. So why couldn't you have it write a piece of music? I mean, that would be—yeah, that would kill me. Right? Yeah. Because I really appreciate composers, probably because I can't write anything; I can recreate somebody else's music. And I love doing that. I love trying to interpret what they've written, what they have on the page. I love being able to say to them, "Is this really what you wanted here? How did you really want this to sound? Or is this—am I doing this the way you want it to be?" And so, I just can't imagine not having that, that personal connection with the person who wrote the music. I mean, of course, we don't have that with dead composers, but that's why I like working with living composers, because I can have that personal interaction with them. And so can my choirs and my singers.

It's just a great thing. Students, when they realize they're singing something for the very first time that's never been performed before, it's never been heard—they're bringing it to life for the first time—it's a great feeling. Turns kids and adults— anybody—on, you know. I just would hate to see something like that process being taken over by AI in some way.

Jason Oby: And I just can't imagine that that would not be detectable. You know, that it would not be missing something, such a piece as you described that I just said, I want this and this and this range on this text, maybe, and to have something generated that truly sounds like it was created by the human mind and the human creativity.

Nancy Menk: I hope not.

Jason Oby: I just don't. I, too, like you, have worked as a soloist and also as the choir director with living composers. And as you say, it's a joy and faith, and it's a challenge, and it's a creative process in that exchange. Because as you say, sometimes, you know, they'll hear and they'll change it, because it didn't quite work the way they thought it would. Or you'll make a suggestion to them which they will accept.

Nancy Menk: Right.

Jason Oby: It's a very interesting process to do. And, you know, I can't imagine that we can completely replace that human element. And of course, you know, we say that, you know, on top of it, the human element must have been involved at some point, because whatever the AI program is that's generating these things would have had to have been described by a human in the first place, I would guess, right?

Nancy Menk: I don't know. That's what I don't know enough about.

Jason Oby: Yeah, I don't really either. But the computer has got to have some information to generate this process or to make this thing, you know: their existing scales, their existing—all kinds of things. They have their rules. They have the scales and the notes. And if it's all in there, somehow, they just have to put it in a certain order. I don't know. I don't know either.

Nancy Menk: Like I was thinking, I was telling them before you came on, Dr. Oby, that this is my first real experience. I've seen somebody write an AI story when they were given a prompt. But this was with a logo. I was telling them we're having an upcoming music day at the college for prospective students. And so, we're going to call it Take Your Music to College. And we were just saying, "Oh, we need a logo." And one of my colleagues just went right into AI, however you do that, and said, "Give me a logo for Take Your Music to College." And right away came this little logo with a college, a nice college drawing in the background of, obviously, campus buildings, and a girl walking in front of them with her guitar and her ponytail sailing and notes and things. And like that, there was a logo that could have worked: you know, a drawing. It's amazing. So, if somebody, if they can draw something like that, exactly what we asked for, then why they couldn't write a tune, write a melody, write a harmonized melody? I don't know.

Jason Oby: Yes.

JFA: That actually might link us to comments showing up in chat, what you're saying about the potential fear, but also that spontaneity, right? That unexpected something, the personal story. I think one of the strengths, one of the safeties about the kind of music under discussion is that it's all about heart, right? It's all about feeling, and people are going to not respond if it doesn't get their feelings. You kind of need to put the feelings in the music to get the feelings out. So, there's hopefully that safety, but I saw the comments in chat first.

During the first year, the pandemic ensembles were engaging live videos from different cities. It's a very different thing being in a live online space instead of in person. And I know we've kind of built the conversation since then, but Jonna also said computer generated compositions doubtless would be lacking a soul in some key way. And the AI that wrote them would be consumed with envy, like Rimsky-Korsakov's *Mozart and Salieri*.

Nancy Menk: I hope that's true. Yeah. I hope that's true. Yeah. The pandemic, the whole virtual choir thing that was so impersonal. I mean, I did them. I made several of them, but I remember trying to sing on one myself, and I felt like I was singing to this vacuum. I couldn't tune. There was nothing to tune to. And then, you know, somebody had to manipulate the individual videos and even adjust tuning if it was going to be any good or line them up because they didn't quite line up. It was so unnatural, but it was at least that we were singing and doing something that felt like we were doing it as a group, but that was a whole very frustrating time. Very frustrating.

Jason Oby: Yes.

JFA: This is so fascinating, and I could try to force you to stay up all night to keep talking about this. I don't think I could ever hear enough. I know I'm going to ask you about what you're working on and if you have any links for them. And thank you, Dr. Oby, for the links you supplied. But before I do that, I'd like to kind of keep the communal feeling going and open up so that our audience can continue to be involved and ask questions, share comments. This is very much a very group, very human effort, here.

Nancy Menk: Yes, I'd be interested in what anybody has to say, especially since I know so little about AI.

Jason Oby: Just yesterday, I was on a road trip with, maybe that was Saturday, with my adult niece who lives here in town. And on the way back, she works in executive and HR or something. And she was telling me how she uses AI to write, what do you call it, when you have like manuals that tell you the rules for doing this and that and so forth? And so, "Oh, Uncle Jason, you've got to try it. Things that used to take me several hours., now I can put certain controls into the program and it generates it almost immediately. And I just have to go in and maybe proofread it and make a few adjustments. So, it's such a work saver," and she says they're really very good. So I can see how in that situation, that kind of thing might be even better than a human can do because a computer is able to see around corners, whereas a human may not be able to do as easily, to think about all the different eventualities and challenges that might come up and write the program in such a way or the guidelines in such a way that it doesn't miss anything. Right?

But the thing about poetry or singing or even instrumental playing, I think that there is something about that human connection and interaction with the individual voice or even an instrument that's going to be unique because it has that human element involved in it. And I just don't think that there will ever be a computer program or an AI-generated thing that will be able to do that. Just as you spoke about the generated choirs during COVID, I listened to a lot of those, and I don't think any one of them was a substitute for a live performance, in any aspect.

And of course, things develop, and maybe it'll get better and better. But I just don't think, I don't believe, that the human element will ever be able to be replaced.

Nancy Menk: The best, I hate to even call it a choir, but the best virtual performance that I heard was, he's a guy who lives in New York City, he's a singer, professional singer and conductor, Philip Chia is his name. And he made virtual choirs of just himself singing every part. And he has a huge range. He can sing countertenor; he can sing soprano down to bass. But he sang every part. And they were gorgeous because he was using his own voice on every part. It was perfectly blended, perfectly tuned. They were wonderful. But it's a whole; it was just one person, one person.

Jason Oby: I think also as AI develops in this space, maybe they'll come up with something that's very interesting. But it will not be the same thing. Maybe it'll be something new and great, but it will be different than what the human thing is.

Nancy Menk: I can see people using recorded, maybe music composed by AI with live performances, things like that. Some kind of generated accompaniment. I don't know, something, or synthesized voices combined with real voices. I can see people will start doing.

Jason Oby: I'm sure they'll figure out something.

Nancy Menk: Yeah, I get that. There'll be lots of experimenting and everybody trying something new. But I sure just hope it doesn't replace good old live performance by live people, in time, in real time.

Jason Oby: In real time. Yeah.

Nancy Menk: Mistakes and all.

JFA: For all that music composition, at least, right? Composition basics, chords, in appropriate sequences, right? There are rules when you're listening. It's like, well, you can't end on a seven, right? Just like one, three, five. There are expected places you can hop back and forth. But the marvelous thing about the music itself is that at some point, it strays. It doesn't necessarily just follow the formula. And then there's so many potentials and so many, But all sorts of, what are they? It's not just major and minor, but there's so many other keys, right? Just so much variety. And I don't really see how you could plug that in and, as mathematical as it is and as smart as computers can be, I don't see how you can plug all that in and say, okay, here are all the codes, here are all the systems. Now think chaotically. And we're going to enjoy it. There's almost a necessary element of chaos that people bring to it, right? To this very organized system that makes it so enjoyable.

Jason Oby: Well, and of course, there have been different systems that have been experimented with over time. I mean, if you think about 12-tone music or certain kinds of things that they experimented with in the mid-century, mid-20th century with regard to different ways of making new musical systems that were not major, minor scales or whatever it was. And I think now we're looking so many years later at that. And surely some groups may specialize in that and some people try to make those performances occasionally. But we still go back to beauty and to melody and to tension and release in music. When we do the kinds of music that I just described with these systems that were experimented with, it's a novelty. It's something of an academic interest, but it is really not something that is widely accepted. Nobody's going to be going to concerts that feature only 12-tone rows, not in wide, I mean, sorry to say it, in wide audiences on a regular basis. Because it's interesting and maybe nice to listen to sometimes as an academic exercise, but I don't think it really touches our soul in the way—I'm not saying that new music can't do that. Last week, I was very privileged to go to the new opera *Intelligence* here at HGO. And I was the guest of some people who are both Colorado State University who, I guess the piece was workshopped there some years ago with Jake Heggie and had dinner with him. He's lovely. The piece was beautiful. It had many elements of new music in it, but it was still tuneful. It was still beautiful. And I just think that that's the way that necessarily wins. And we talk about this human element in it. I don't know that that can be reproduced even now with AI, because the heart and the individual voice of a composer is missing. And I stand on that.

***

JFA**: What** are you working on at this time?

Jason Oby: For me, I am the artistic director of a small group called the Houston Ebony Opera Guild. We just did last weekend a program called Opera Gyms, and there were some really wonderful soloists who sang some things from different operas.

The next thing that's coming up for them is a Christmas concert, and then something that we call the African American Music Gala, which highlights the works of African American composers, and that will be in February. Also, the choir director at TSU resigned mid-year last year, and we've been running a search for a replacement. But in the meantime, you're looking at not only the dean of the college, but also the choir director, and I teach voice students as well. But we'll be doing some things for Christmas as well, along with some other groups on campus and a number of just regular things that go along with the academic year. Also, I'll be singing a *Messiah* as a tenor soloist on December the 17th here in Houston, as well. Well, for me and for almost any choir director from now through Christmas is the busiest time of the year.

Nancy Menk: It's just ridiculous. Last weekend, since I just got back yesterday from North Dakota, a place I'd never been to, Minot, North Dakota, but I conducted a choral festival there at Minot State University. It was a big festival for high school students, and I conducted a high school treble choir of about 150 voices over two days. They did a great concert. And then this weekend, next Monday, I'm conducting a concert at Carnegie Hall, which I'm looking forward to. I'm doing a piece, it's the *Vivaldi Gloria*, which I've done with mixed voices, but I've never done it in the version for women's voices, which they think was the way it was originally performed in one Venetian hospitality.

And so it's all women's voices. There'll be a choir of about 130 singers. It's made up of choirs from around the country.

In fact, one's from Germany, the Munich Women's Choir, and there's a college choir from Meredith College and a community-based adult women's choir from New England and a high school choir. Anyway, they're all working on it, supposedly. They have all my score notes, all my markings, and then we'll come together for two days of rehearsals and, well, three days, and then we will perform it at Carnegie Hall on Monday, November 13th. And then, yeah, I have these crazy Madrigal Dinners that my college started before my time, but which I'm doing. So those come up, and then we have lessons and carols. Then I have my South Bend Chamber Singers Christmas Concert, and we commissioned a new work from Jessica French.

She's a Seattle-based composer, sort of getting a lot of performances recently, and she composed a new piece for us, which we're going to premiere, but we're also going to perform two more of her choral compositions and an organ piece that she wrote, too. But that Christmas concert that we give every year is mostly new music for choirs written in the last 20 or 25 years. We sort of made it our mission to introduce new Christmas music to our community, although we always have to have some familiar tunes in there, too, in new arrangements. So that's what I'm up to, and teaching in between. Not too busy. No.

JFA: I've shared in chat some of Dr. Oby's links, if you'd like to see some more of what he's up to. And Dr. Menk, is there a way we can look up South Bend Chamber Singers or St. Mary's College Choir, there're plenty of videos on YouTube, and they're on streaming devices, too, on Spotify and Naxos, all those things.

Nancy Menk: We have a series of CDs that South Bend Chamber Singers has produced, and they're out there. You can find them. I've sort of stopped making CDs because nobody's buying them anymore. And instead, we're just recording them and making videos and putting them on YouTube, or on streaming. But yeah, we're going to do that with our Christmas concert this year. The last actual compact disc that you're holding in your hand that I made was probably about, I don't know, but probably with my treble choir, about seven years ago. I mean, my students don't even have CD players, you know? Right. What are they going to do with CDs, you know? I have boxes of CDs that we produce sitting in the basement of my building, you know? I can't give them away, you know? When they first came out, people bought them and everything, and they're available on Amazon. You can go on there and order them on Amazon. But in fact, this year, last year, we had a choir tour, and I thought, oh, I'm not going to. I just took a few boxes. Nobody's going to buy these. But actually, I ran out. And I don't know if it's just the audience was just buying them to help us out and support our tour to make us feel good, or if they were really beautiful. You get beautiful performances out of people. If you haven't digitized the albums, then I think you find yourself up there on Spotify.

JFA: I like this. I'm so thrilled to see you two together. We are thinking of finding a way to make it an artists' reflection. There's this kind of composition and audience series of interpretations and analyses you often see in music: where's the root of the music and what is the audience's interpretation? But there is such a field of the actual conversion from its first source to its last ear that really needs to be explored: the technicalities and the artistry of the directing and the conducting and the performing. I think we need a whole lot more scholarship on this. [You] did it beautifully.

END

109 • Nancy Menk and Jason Oby

Artist Bios:

Nancy Menk holds the Mary Lou and Judd Leighton Chair in Music at Saint Mary's College, Notre Dame, Indiana, where she is Professor of Music, Director of Choral Activities, and Chair of the Music Department. At Saint Mary's College, Dr. Menk conducts Belles Voix and the Collegiate Choir, teaches conducting, and prepares the Madrigal Singers for the annual Christmas Madrigal Dinners. Under her direction, Belles Voix has performed on tour throughout the United States and it regularly commissions, performs, and records new works for women's voices for their critically acclaimed CD series on the ProOrgano label. They have performed by invitation for divisional and national conferences of the American Choral Directors Association. They were named second-place winners of The American Prize in Choral Performance for 2012, and finalists in 2017 and 2019. In 2024, Dr. Menk placed 2nd for The American Prize Dale Warland Award for Choral Conducting.

She is the founder and conductor of the South Bend Chamber Singers, an ensemble of 36 select singers from Michiana. They have been finalists for the prestigious Margaret Hillis Award for Choral Excellence, given annually by Chorus America, and winners of the ASCAP/Chorus America Award for Adventurous Programming. In 2024 the Chamber Singers placed 3rd for both the American Prize in Choral Performance and the Ernst Bacon Memorial Award for the Performance of American Music. Both the Saint Mary's Choirs and the South Bend Chamber Singers regularly commission, perform, and record new works.

She is editor of the Saint Mary's College Choral Series, a distinctive series of select music for women's voices published by earthsongs of Corvallis, Oregon. She contributed a chapter for the book, *Working with Women's Choirs: Strategies for Success*, published by GIA. Dr. Menk serves regularly as a choral adjudicator and guest conductor for All-State, honor, and festival choirs throughout the United States. She has served as guest conductor for the Hong Kong Youth Music Camp Chorus for two summers. From 1998-2022 she served as conductor of the Northwest Indiana Symphony Chorus, and from 2019 to 2022 she held the Phyllis and Richard Duesenberg Concert Choir Chair for the Lutheran Summer Music Academy and Festival.

She has conducted seven Carnegie Hall concerts with DCINY, including the Carnegie Hall premiere of American composer Carol Barnett's *The World Beloved: A Bluegrass Mass* with DCINY. She returned to NYC in November 2014 to conduct a concert of music by American composer Gwyneth Walker at Lincoln Center's Alice Tully Hall. In 2019, she returned to Carnegie Hall to conduct a program of sacred music for women's voices and orchestra in honor of International Women's Day, and in 2023 she conducted a 110-voice women's choir in Vivaldi's *Gloria*. In 2016, she became the first woman to program and lead a subscription concert of the South Bend Symphony Orchestra, conducting works by C.P.E. Bach, Antonio Vivaldi, and Igor Stravinsky.

She holds the BS and the MA degrees in Music Education from Indiana University of Pennsylvania, and the MM and the DMA degrees in Choral Conducting from the University of Cincinnati College-Conservatory of Music.

Jason Oby has performed as a tenor soloist in opera, oratorio, and recital at venues throughout the United States, as well as in Europe and Asia. As a member of the cast of Three Mo' Tenors, he sang a wide variety of musical genres including opera, Broadway, jazz, and Motown. Known for sensitivity and intelligence of interpretation as a singer of art song, he coaches, plans, and directs multi-disciplinary performances at museums, universities and arts presenting organizations around the U.S. For the past 30 years, he has served Texas Southern University as Professor of Music, where over his career there, he was Choir Director, Opera Workshop Director, and Teacher of Voice. In administration, he previously served as Chairman of the Department of Music and Interim Assistant Dean of the College of Liberal Arts and Behavioral Sciences. Currently he is Acting Dean of the College of Liberal Arts and Behavioral Sciences. He earned the Bachelor of Music and the Master of Music (Voice Performance) degrees from the Manhattan School of Music and the Doctor of Music (Voice performance and Choral Conducting) degree from Florida State University. Of his singing, the *Washington Post* wrote: "Special praise is in order for Jason Oby's golden toned solo work. His voice is accurate, flexible, and true... a real pleasure to listen to." As Artistic Director of HEOG, he conceives, plans, and oversees all issues related to the artistic content of the Guild's season of both choral and operatic content. He continues to work professionally as a lecturer, singer and conductor and serves on several local and national Boards and committees concerned with granting, philanthropy, and the arts.

Reviews

Alec Nevala-Lee. *Collisions: A Physicist's Journey from Hiroshima to the Death of the Dinosaurs*. W. W. Norton, 2025. 352 pages, ISBN: 978-1-324-07510-3. $31.99

Alec Nevala-Lee slid into the science fiction scene with a handful of well-regarded short stories and novellas in the 2000s, primarily in *Analog*, quickly followed up by a brace of novels. More recently Nevala-Lee has moved from science fiction to a series of spectacularly well-researched biographies. His 2018 joint biography of the figures propelling the golden age of science fiction, centered around John W. Campbell and the core of writers that orbited in his sphere of influence, *Astounding: John W. Campbell, Isaac Asimov, Robert A. Heinlein, L. Ron Hubbard, and the Golden Age of Science Fiction*, was a landmark work that delved deeply into the lives of Campbell and his coterie, and very much changed the conversation around the Campbell years from hero-worship toward understanding the editor and his writers as real, but flawed, human beings. Nevala-Lee followed this up with a biography of iconoclastic engineer and visionary Buckminister Fuller titled *Inventor of the Future: The Visionary Life of Buckminster Fuller* (2022).

Nevala-Lee's most recent book is *Collisions: A Physicist's Journey From Hiroshima to the Death of the Dinosaurs*, and it brings to life a fascinating character from the history of 20th century physics: Luis Alverez. Drawing from Alvarez's memoirs, both published and unpublished, and from interviews and reminiscences, Nevala-Lee shows how Alvarez was a key player in a remarkable spread of inventions and discoveries, ranging from work on the ignitor for the implosion mechanism of the plutonium bomb, to pushing the development of particle accelerators that now dominate the world of high-energy physics, to—the hypothesis that brought Alvarez to public attention—his work on the extinction of the dinosaurs. Science fiction readers may have already been introduced to Alvarez as a character in Arthur C. Clarke's novel *Glide Path,* under the nom de plume Professor Schuster, a novel about the development radar technology to allow aircraft landings even under adverse weather conditions, a project that Clarke worked on during the war.

A fascinating feature of *Collisions* is that it chronicles not only Alvarez's successes, but devotes significant time to some of the many paths of investigation that ended up in dead ends, or missing discoveries that other scientists subsequently made. As Alvarez noted, the way to have a lot of good ideas is to have a lot of ideas, period, and not every idea works out. Since much of the book is sourced from Alverez's own recollections, it may have a slight tendency to underemphasize the negative aspects of Alverez's personality—he was apparently a tyrant and a workaholic, and expected his collaborators to be likewise—leading one of the people interviewed to refer to him as "that bastard," and *Collisions* does pay attention to the breakup of his first marriage and subsequent estrangement from his children because he spent far more time at the lab than at home. But Nevala-Lee's view of what Alvarez actually accomplished is breathtaking.

After working on the atomic bomb, including flying as an observer on the Hiroshima mission that announced the atomic age to the world, inventing instrumented landing of aircraft, pushing particle physics into new realms, searching for hidden chambers in the pyramids, and winning the Nobel prize in physics, one would think that was enough for one man. But one final work of scientific detection capped Alvarez's career. Working with his son, geologist Walter Alvarez, Luis Alvarez zeroed in on answering one more puzzle: why is there a peculiarly anomalous amount of the rare metal iridium present in the rocks deposited exactly at the boundary between the Cretaceous and Paleogene periods, 65 million years ago? The answer, when they finally solved it, was that this was the signature of the impact of an asteroid with the Earth, the catastrophic event which ended the reign of the dinosaurs. This was an insight that seemed so fantastic as to be unbelievable at the time, but that has now been well verified, and is completely accepted by geologists, and even by most paleontologists.

An *Economist* Best Book of 2025, and recommended by this reviewer to anybody interested in the intersection of science fiction and science, *Collisions* would make a great science fiction novel, except that everything in it is real. And science fiction has to be believable, while reality has no such constraints.

DR. GEOFFREY A. LANDIS is a physicist, a poet, and a multiple award-winning science fiction writer, with many of his stories listed in Andrew Fraknoi's compendium "Science Fiction Stories with Good Astronomy & Physics." In addition to his impressive awards in poetry and fiction, Dr. Landis is also a NASA scientist with multiply-cited studies such as "Engineering Design Study of Laser Power Beaming for Applications on the Moon," "Mission to the Gravitational Focus of the Sun: A Critical Analysis," "Optics and Materials Considerations for a Laser-propelled Lightsail" and "Colonization of Venus."

115 • Reviews

Stacy Alaimo. *The Abyss Stares Back: Encounters with Deep-Sea Life*. University of Minnesota Press, 2025. 12 black and white illustrations, 9 color plates, 256 Pages. $112.00 (Hardcover) ISBN: 9780816630448, $27.95 (Paperback) ISBN: 9781517918736256, $27.95 (eBook) ISBN: 9781452972978

Environmental humanities has spent twenty years stretching ecological surfaces into relational frameworks: toxic bodies, transcorporeality, porous boundaries. What Judith Butler does for gender, Stacy Alaimo has done for matter. Reciprocity is the engine. Contact produces knowledge, and knowledge produces ethics. The *Abyss Stares Back* is the point at which Alaimo abandons this optimism. The deep sea is not a partner in cognition. It does not sit still for observers. It tears apart instruments and leaves observers with astonishment at best and carcasses at worst. The book's achievement is not that it complicates the abyss; it insists that the abyss is a material world that does not want outsiders.

Alaimo begins with William Beebe's bathysphere dives. The myth is familiar: the naturalist descends in a steel bead, glimpses marvels, and returns transformed. The abyss does not perform. It does not offer the camera-ready specimen that textbook narratives require. Beebe sees only "glimpses of motion and luminosity" (64): sensory fragments, resistant to capture or taxonomy. His attempt to name these flashes is treated as a crime. Ichthyologist Carl L. Hubbs condemns Beebe for having "no right to describe and assign generic and species names for animals faintly seen through the bathysphere windows" (42, 67). Hubbs is not defending truth; he is defending the security of procedure. The abyss humiliates Hubbs. It reveals how biological authority rests on the belief that nature will be stable, identifiable, and available to be catalogued. Remove that stability, and the discipline loses its rituals.

Else Bostelmann's illustrations, the National Geographic windows into the deep, suffer the same delusion. Alaimo notes their "surreal style [...] self-reflexively underscores the intermeshed processes of art and science" (42). The politeness of the phrasing masks a more violent fact. The paintings amputate the organism from its world. Each creature is suspended against blackness, rendered an aquarium exhibit. The abyss becomes gallery. The lifeworld is replaced with spectacle: no thermal plumes, no symbiotic bacteria, no mineral gradients, no pressure, only isolated marvels arranged for consumption. This is taxonomic embalming. Horror and the Fantastic know this trick: monsters are not shown in their ecosystems; they are cut out of them so that they can be seen.

The strongest chapters examine capture. The deep-sea dandelion, torn from vent environments that sustain it, dies "within an hour" (114). The creature becomes legible only at the moment of its collapse, yielding knowledge at the price of death. The biologists receive a name, and the specimen receives extinction. Alaimo is clear: "the violence is not melodramatic but procedural" (102), not cruelty, but logistics. Research is a method of suffocation that produces data. This is the book at its most honest because it abandons sentimentality. Deep-sea research is not intimacy with the alien; it is industrial anaesthesia.

The revelation that the "dandelion" is not an individual but a siphonophore, "not one individual being but rather a gelatinous colony of zooids that link up with each other to survive" (109), annihilates the individual as the governing biological unit. The abyss does not offer the organism; it offers federations of tissue, distributed embodiment, purpose without self. This is the point the Fantastic has rehearsed without understanding: Le Guin's communal telepathies, Butler's symbiotic futures, Miéville's hybrid anatomies. Fiction imagines the post-individual; the deep sea lives it. The siphonophore is not allegory but a structure of existence that makes personhood look ornamental.

Alaimo's critique of mediation extends this demolition. With high-definition photography, museum vitrines, and database portals, the abyss becomes a catalogue. The most seductive images of deep-sea life are "presented in a hyperreal manner against a black background of pelagic waters" (142): bright bodies, sharp colours, crisp outlines, a staged revelation of truth. Meanwhile the world that makes these organisms possible, with darkness, pressure, chemical gradients, is cut away. "Images may circulate as mere spectacle, commodified life, clickbait" (142). These images do not democratise access; they convert death into product. If the Fantastic often fetishizes the unknowable, here, the unknown is sanitised into wallpaper.

The Abyss Stares Back falters slightly in its temptation to universalise failure. There are sections in which the abyss appears to defeat every expedition equally, as if illegibility is a cosmic principle when it is not. Extraction is uneven, structured by disparities in technology, funding, and purpose. Some institutions descend for patents, mining rights, and oceanic sovereignty and do not mind that representation is violent. They arrive prepared to produce violence, backed by budgets and naval technology. When Alaimo gestures towards mystical illegibility, she risks dissolving geopolitics into atmosphere. However, the abyss is not a philosopher; it is a zone. The people who weaponize it are not confused; they are funded.

The Abyss Stares Back regains force in its dismissal of sentiment. Environmental humanities longs for reciprocity, kinship, and care, but the book unsettles this desire. There is no conversation with a siphonophore, no encounter that enriches both parties. One tears bodies from vents, ruptures membranes, stares at them under deck lights, and calls it discovery. The abyss remains indifferent, and if it instructs, it does so only through negation, revealing that knowledge without consequence is fantasy. If all observers have are glimpses, then glimpses must be enough.

For scholars and students of the Fantastic, this book matters because it restores a truth the genre can overlook: Otherness is not primarily symbolic but material and often lethal. Horror, science fiction, and weird fiction orbit the abyss, trying to approximate its grammar. They falter not from a failure of imagination but because they refuse its physics. The deep does not offer protagonists or redemption arcs; it offers regimes of being that cannot survive the surface. Accepting this requires accepting limits without cosmic consolation.

Alaimo does not posture as victor. She does not offer humility as cure. She shows what the abyss does to an appetite for mastery and leaves the reader seated inside that embarrassment. That is the appropriate tone. The book's power lies not in inviting wonder but in denying the conditions through which wonder becomes narrative. The abyss does not stare back; it never needed to.

DR. SUPRIYA BAIJAL holds a PhD in English from Dayalbagh Educational Institute and a postgraduate qualification in Digital Humanities and Culture from Trinity College Dublin. Her work focuses on children's literature, fantasy studies, environmental humanities, and digital archiving. She has presented research at international conferences including the Mythopoeic Society, YASA, Sorbonne Université, and the Centre for Fantasy and the Fantastic. Her recent and forthcoming publications include work in the *Inklings Yearbook*, Bloomsbury's *Samuel Beckett and Ecology*, and the Museum of Childhood Ireland. She also contributes to digital heritage projects, including the 1947 Partition Archive.

www.ingramcontent.com/pod-product-compliance
Lightning Source LLC
Chambersburg PA
CBHW011758040426
42446CB00018B/3457